EDITOR: Maryanne Blacker

FOOD EDITOR: Pamela Clark

• • •

DESIGNER: Robbylee Phelan

HOME ECONOMISTS: Barbara Northwood,
Laura Robertson, Lucy Clayton, Wendy Berecry,
Allyson Mitchell

KITCHEN ASSISTANT: Amy Wong

• • •

FOOD STYLIST: Jacqui Hing

PHOTOGRAPHER: Russell Brooks

• • •

HOME LIBRARY STAFF:

ASSISTANT EDITOR: Beverley Hudec

DESIGNER: Paula Wooller

EDITORIAL COORDINATOR: Lara Quinlin

• • •

ACP PUBLISHER: Richard Walsh

ACP ASSOCIATE PUBLISHER: Bob Neil

• • •

Produced by The Australian Women's Weekly Home Library.
Typeset by Photoset Computer Service Pty Ltd, and Letter
Perfect, Sydney. Printed by Dai Nippon Co., Ltd in Japan.
Published by Australian Consolidated Press,
54 Park Street Sydney.
♦ **AUSTRALIA:** Distributed by Network Distribution Company,
54 Park Street Sydney, (02) 282 8777.
♦ **UNITED KINGDOM:** Distributed in the U.K. by Australian
Consolidated Press (UK) Ltd, 20 Galowhill Rd, Brackmills,
Northampton NN4 OEE (0604) 760 456.
♦ **CANADA:** Distributed in Canada by Whitecap
Books Ltd, 1086 West 3rd St,
North Vancouver V7P 3J6 (604) 980 9852.
♦ **NEW ZEALAND:** Distributed in New Zealand by Netlink
Distribution Company, 17B Hargreaves St, Level 5,
College Hill, Auckland 1 (9) 302 7616.
♦ **SOUTH AFRICA:** Distributed in South Africa by Intermag,
PO Box 57394, Springfield 2137 (011) 493 3200.
ACN 000 031 747.

• • •

Microwave Cookbook

Includes index.
ISBN 0 949892 28 9.

1. Microwave cookery. (Series: Australian
Women's Weekly Home Library).

641.5'882

• • •

© A C P 1992 (Reprint)
This publication is copyright. No part of it may be reproduced
or transmitted in any form without the written permission
of the publishers.

• • •

COVER: At back from left: Strawberry Jam, Processor Lemon
Marmalade, page 78, Dried Apricot and Passionfruit
Conserve, page 79, Vegetable Risotto, page 67, Curried Kiwi
Clam Soup, page 21, Moist Carrot Cake, page 76, Almond
Brittle, Butterscotch Brazil Nuts, page 82, Chocolate Cream
Cheesecake, page 89. At front from left: Beef with Black Bean
Sauce, page 46, Tomato Mozzarella Chicken, page 33,
Meatloaf with Cheese and Pepper Topping, page 46,
Mini Terrines with Red Currant Glaze, page 53.
OPPOSITE: Clockwise from bottom: Bean-stuffed Onions,
page 60, Creamy Basil Chokoes, page 64, Chinese Vegetables
in Sate Sauce, page 59, Vegetarian Moussaka, page 66,
Asparagus with Curry Hollandaise, page 68.

...ompted...
...to two sect...
microv...s, includes a...cipes. The...
section, which starts on pa...4, for CONVECTION/
MICROWAVE ovens and contains 70 recipes.

Pamela Clark

FOOD EDITOR

L.I.T. Library

3 9002 10036141 0

BRITISH & NORTH AMERICAN READERS: Please note that Australian cup
and spoon measurements are metric. Conversion charts for cup and spoon
measurements and oven temperatures appear on page 5.
A glossary explaining unfamiliar terms and ingredients appears on page 4.

USEFUL INFORMATION 850 w

This cookbook is a recipe book with helpful hints in each section and on this and the next page we have included some extra general information on microwave ovens. It is important you read the instruction manual that accompanies your oven.

Commonsense is the main requirement when using a microwave oven. They are safe, easy to use, economical and time-saving. They heat the food, not the oven or kitchen, and cut down on washing up — you will end up cooking lots of things in serving dishes.

The difference between microwave cooking and conventional cooking is that microwaves act on the molecules in the food immediately the door is shut and the power is on. Conventional (like CONVECTIONAL) cooking involves heating the food before it starts to cook.

A convection oven operates in exactly the same way as a fan-forced oven and gives the same result in cooking as a conventional oven.

Domestic microwave ovens at present on the market vary in watt output, roughly between 500 and 700 watts. All the recipes in this book were tested on a 600-watt oven. If your oven has a higher or lower output than 600 watts, add or deduct a little cooking time to the recipe.

The oven we used had quite a lot of settings. We have tried to use HIGH in most recipes in this book — presuming everyone is in a hurry. However, the MEDIUM is about 70 per cent power, MEDIUM HIGH 90 per cent and MEDIUM LOW 50 per cent power. If your oven has HIGH and DEFROST only you will have to start on HIGH and go back to DEFROST to continue cooking.

It is difficult to distribute microwave energy evenly in the oven, so some ovens have stirrers, distributors, or turntables, so the food is rotated. It is also the reason behind stirring during cooking. Some food cannot be stirred, so these dishes are rotated and/or rearranged.

Cooking times depend on the amount of food in the microwave oven, e.g. 1 small potato will cook on HIGH in about 4 minutes, 4 small potatoes will take about 6 minutes. Times given in our recipes are only for your guidance. Always check food after minimum suggested cooking time.

EQUIPMENT TO USE

If in doubt about the suitability of a dish or plate, etc., for use in a microwave oven, stand the dish in the oven with a glass of water next to it. Turn the control to HIGH, set for a minute. If the dish remains cold, it is fine for use, if (like the water) it gets hot don't use it in the microwave oven.

Food will cook more evenly and faster in a shallow, straight-sided round or oval dish rather than in a deeper dish of the same capacity.

Microwaveproof ring pans give good cooking results as the energy penetrates the food from all sides as well as the centre. You can make your own "ring tin" by placing a glass in the centre of an ovenproof dish — see picture below.

There is some new equipment made from a light, durable plastic which will soon be available in Australia. It will be suitable to use in a MICROWAVE, CONVECTION and conventional oven and will withstand freezing and then cooking at high temperatures in the oven.

There is an excellent range of disposable microwaveproof equipment available in supermarkets that can be used several times. There is a well-designed roaster rack that will fit inside a casserole dish. There is also a cooking sheet/pizza pan which is good for placing over the turntable to catch any spills.

Browning utensils are also available. They have a surface which can be heated in the microwave oven, then the food is placed on the surface to brown. We have not used them in this book, because we wanted to use equipment that was easy to find in most kitchens.

Do not use dishes with metal trim or handles, etc., fine crystal or Melamine® or Centura® bowls or plates.

Styrofoam®, plastic storage and icecream containers can be used for reheating some food as long as it is not too high in butter, oil, sugar or honey content. The food, when hot, will distort the plastic. Don't use these containers to cook raw food.

Foil food trays can be used if they are at least two thirds full. Keep trays about 2.5cm away from walls and door of oven.

Aluminium foil is useful in the microwave oven as it reflects microwave energy. Use it to cover thinner parts of food — e.g., the ends

of chicken drumsticks or wings, the corners of square or rectangular dishes where food will cook first. The foil reflects the waves away and stops the already cooked food from drying out. Wrap the foil tightly around the food when covering so that pieces of foil do not protrude.

We used plastic food wrap to cover foods when necessary; allow a little vent for steam to escape, as shown. Be careful of steam when

removing food wrap — do this away from you, as shown. Cover food in the microwave oven, if you would cover it when cooked conventionally or if you want to retain moisture. Always cover food when reheating.

Oven bags are good to use in the microwave oven, secure them loosely, either with a rubber band, string, or a strip cut from the top of the bag. Do not use paper, plastic or foil-covered metal "ties".

Use absorbent kitchen paper to stand pies, buns, breads, croissants, etc., on for reheating. The paper absorbs moisture from the steam created and helps prevent sogginess. Rashers of bacon are best cooked between sheets of paper; this stops splattering.

COOKING TIMES, TIPS

It is difficult to be precise in timing, as identical ovens vary slightly — as do conventional ovens. The golden rule is to UNDERCOOK all food, check to see if it is done to your liking and return it to the oven if necessary. Remember, 30 seconds or less can mean the difference between food being properly cooked or not.

As you become more experienced and confident using the appliance you will also become accurate in estimating the timing.

Standing time is important, follow instructions carefully. Some food continues to cook after it is taken from the oven.

The diagrams, at right, show you how to position food in the microwave oven whether or not you have a turntable. Some ovens have inbuilt microwave stirrers or distributors to spread the microwaves; this can eliminate or minimise turning of food during cooking.

For even cooking: buy fish, chicken, vegetables of similar size and thickness. Chop meat and vegetables, etc., evenly.

Foods which have thick and thin ends such as fish, chicken, asparagus, etc., should have the thick ends placed toward the walls of the microwave oven, either in a dish or on the turntable.

We have deliberately left salt out of most of our recipes. You will find the flavor of food more intense when cooked in the microwave oven. It is

wise to season lightly with any herbs, sauce or flavoring after cooking or standing time but this depends on the recipe.

We have specified beef or chicken stock throughout this book. You have a choice either to make your own (see how to make a simple chicken stock on page 21) or to use stock cubes. One stock cube to 1 cup water will give you a fairly well flavored stock. Make allowances for the salt content of the stock cubes.

We have not used any commercial browning agents in the recipes in this book. There are quite a number of them available in supermarkets; they do color food and make it look as if it were cooked in a conventional oven. We have, however, used paprika, soy sauce, worcestershire sauce and cinnamon to color the food slightly for appearance sake. These ingredients are specified in individual recipes.

Don't deep or shallow fry in the microwave oven; the oil temperature cannot be controlled. And don't boil eggs.

Pierce membranes of food with skewer or fork — eggs (white and yolk) potatoes and tomatoes, etc.

Diagrams show positioning of food or dishes on turntable or large plate in base of oven. For best results food and dishes should be evenly spaced and at least 2.5cm apart.

EXTRA TIPS

Use your microwave for:

- Heating well wrung out hand towels on HIGH 1 minute.
- Drying herb and flowers on HIGH until dry.
- Warming baby's bottle.
- Drying fresh breadcrumbs.
- Dissolving gelatine.
- Melting chocolate, butter, jam, honey, liquid glucose, etc.
- Continuing to cook an underdone boiled egg (with top cut off and replaced — this will take only a few seconds).
- Softening too-hard icecream.
- Recrisping stale biscuits and potato crisps breakfast cereals, etc., on paper — HIGH, 45 to 60 seconds.
- Warming citrus fruit to obtain more juice — HIGH, 20 to 30 seconds, stand few minutes before squeezing.
- Softening cream cheese and butter.
- Heating brandy, etc., for flaming — HIGH, 15 to 30 seconds, pour over food, ignite carefully.
- Individual serves of coffee, mulled wine, soups, hot chocolate, Irish Coffee, etc.

GLOSSARY

Alcohol: is optional but gives a particular flavour. You can use fruit juice or water instead to make up the liquid content required.

Bacon Rashers: bacon slices

Bean Sprouts: mung bean sprouts; these should be topped and tailed.

Benedictine: brandy-based liqueur, flavoured with honey and herbs.

Bicarbonate of Soda: baking soda.

Biscuits: also known as cookies.

Nice: sugar-topped plain sweet biscuits, ideal for crumbs.

Black Beans: are fermented, salted soy beans, use canned or dried. Drain and rinse canned variety, soak and rinse dried variety, leftover beans will keep for months in an airtight container in the refrigerator. Mash beans when cooking to release the flavour.

Breadcrumbs:
Stale: use 1 or 2 day old white bread made into crumbs by grating, blending or processing.
Packaged Dry: use fine packaged breadcrumbs.

Butter: use salted or unsalted (sweet) butter; 125g is equal to 1 stick butter.

Buttermilk: is now made by adding a culture to skim milk to give a slightly acid flavour; skim milk can be substituted.

Chicken: size is determined by a numbering system; for example no. 13 is a 1.3 kg bird, a no. 10 is 1kg. This system applies to most poultry.

Chillies: are available in many different types and sizes. The small ones (bird's eye or bird peppers) are the hottest. Use tight rubber gloves when chopping fresh chillies as they can burn your skin. The seeds are the hottest part of the chillies so remove them if you want to reduce the heat content of recipes.

Chinese Barbecued Pork: roasted pork fillets available from many Asian food and specialty stores.

Chinese Dried Mushrooms: unique in flavour; soak in hot water, covered, for 20 minutes, drain. Remove and discard stems, use caps as indicated in recipes.

Chocolate:
Dark: we used good quality cooking chocolate.

Chokoes: also known as chayote and christophenes.

Chorizo Sausages: Spanish and Mexican highly spiced pork sausages seasoned with garlic, cayenne pepper, chilli, etc. They are ready to eat when bought. If unavailable, use a hot spicy type of salami.

Coconut: use desiccated coconut unless otherwise specified.

Copha: a solid white shortening based on coconut oil. Kremelta and Palmin can be substituted.

Cornflour: cornstarch.

Cream: is simply a light pouring cream, also known as half'n'half.
Sour: a thick commercially cultured soured cream.
Sour Light: a less dense commercially cultured soured cream; do not substitute this for sour cream.
Thickened (whipping) Cream: is specified when necessary in recipes.

Cream Cheese: also known as Philly.

Custard Powder: pudding mix.

Eggplant: aubergine.

Five Spice Powder: a pungent mixture of ground spices which includes cinnamon, cloves, fennel, star anise and Szechwan peppers.

Flour:
White Plain: all-purpose flour.
White Self-Raising: substitute plain (all-purpose) flour and baking powder in the proportion of ¾ metric cup plain flour to 2 level metric teaspoons of baking powder. Sift together several times before using. If using 8oz measuring cup, use 1 cup plain flour to 2 level teaspoons baking powder.
Wholemeal: wholewheat flour without baking powder.
Wholemeal Self-Raising (wholewheat): substitute plain wholemeal flour and baking powder as for white flour.

Fresh Herbs: we have specified when to use fresh or dried herbs. We used dried (not ground) herbs in the proportion of 1:4 for fresh herbs. For example: 1 teaspoon dried herbs instead of 4 teaspoons (1 tablespoon) chopped fresh herbs.

Garam Masala: there are many variations of the combinations of cardamom, cinnamon, cloves, coriander, cumin and nutmeg used to make up this spice used often in Indian cooking. Sometimes pepper is used to make a hot variation. Garam masala is available in jars from delicatessens and supermarkets.

Gherkins: cornichons.

Ginger:
Fresh, Green or Root Ginger: scrape away outside skin and grate, chop or slice ginger as required. Fresh, peeled ginger can be preserved with enough dry sherry to cover; keep in jar in refrigerator; it will keep for months.
Glace: fresh ginger root preserved in sugar syrup; crystallised ginger can be substituted; rinse off the sugar with warm water, dry ginger well before using.
Ground: is also available but should not be substituted for fresh ginger.

Golden Syrup: maple, pancake syrup or honey can be substituted.

Grainy Mustard: a French style of textured mustard containing crushed mustard seeds.

Grand Marnier: a brandy-based orange-flavoured liqueur.

Ground Almonds: we used packaged commercially ground nuts in our recipes unless otherwise specified.

Hoisin Sauce: is a thick sweet Chinese barbecue sauce made from a mixture of salted black beans, onion and garlic.

Jam: conserve.

Lemon Butter: also known as lemon curd or lemon cheese.

Liquid Glucose (glucose syrup): made from wheat starch; available at health food stores and supermarkets.

Marsala: a sweet fortified wine.

Minced Steak: ground beef.

Mixed Peel: a mixture of crystallised citrus peel; also known as candied peel.

Mixed Spice: a finely ground combination of spices which includes allspice, nutmeg and cinnamon; used as an ingredient in sweet recipes.

Oil: we used a light polyunsaturated oil throughout this book.

Oyster Sauce: a thick sauce made from oysters cooked in salt and soy sauce.

Parisian Essence: a concentrated liquid brown food colouring.

Peppers: capsicum or bell peppers.

Prawns: also known as shrimp. Most of the recipes in this book use fresh, uncooked (green) prawns.

Prosciutto: uncooked, unsmoked ham, cured in salt.

Punnet: small basket usually holding about 250g fruit.

Rind: zest.

Rum: we used an underproof dark rum.

4

Sate Sauce: a spicy sauce based on soy sauce; it contains sugar, oil, chilli, onion, garlic and shrimp.

Sesame Oil: made from roasted, crushed white sesame seeds, is an aromatic golden-coloured oil with a nutty flavour. It is always used in small quantities and added mostly towards the end of the cooking time. It is not the same as the sesame oil sold in health food stores and should not be used to fry food.

Shallots: also known as spring onions and scallions.

Snow Peas: also known as mange tout, sugar peas or Chinese peas.

Spinach:

English: a soft-leafed vegetable, more delicate in taste than silverbeet (spinach); however, young silverbeet can be substituted for English spinach.

Silverbeet: a large-leafed vegetable, remove white stalk before cooking.

Stock Cubes: available in various flavours. Powdered stock can be used; 1 level teaspoon powdered stock is equivalent to 1 small stock cube.

Sugar: we used coarse granulated table sugar, also known as crystal sugar, unless otherwise specified.

Black: a dark molasses-flavoured sugar, less refined than brown sugar.

Brown: a soft fine granulated sugar with molasses present which gives it its characteristic colour.

Castor: fine granulated table sugar.

Icing Sugar: also known as confectioners' sugar or powdered sugar. We used icing sugar mixture, not pure icing sugar in this book.

Raw: natural light brown granulated sugar or "sugar in the raw".

Sultanas: seedless white raisins.

Tia Maria: coffee-flavoured liqueur.

Tomato Sauce: tomato ketchup.

Tomato Supreme: a canned product consisting of tomatoes, onions, celery, peppers and seasonings.

Vanilla Essence: we used imitation vanilla extract.

Vegeroni: vegetable-flavoured, multi-coloured pasta.

Wheatmeal Biscuits: slightly sweet wholewheat crackers; can be used as a substitute for Graham crackers.

White Fish Fillets: simply means non-oily fish, and could include bream, flathead, whiting, snapper, jewfish and ling. Redfish comes into this category.

Wild Rice: from North America but is not a member of the rice family, it is fairly expensive as it is difficult to cultivate but has a distinctive, delicious nutty flavour.

Zucchini: courgette.

The picture at left shows the equipment we used when we tested the recipes in this book. Apart from the two microwaveproof pans (patty and ring pans) the other items can be found in most kitchens.

Cup and Spoon Measurements

To ensure accuracy in your recipes use the standard metric measuring equipment approved by Standards Australia:

(a) 250 millilitre cup for measuring liquids. A litre jug *(capacity 4 cups)* is also available.

(b) a graduated set of four cups – measuring 1 cup, half, third and quarter cup – for items such as flour, sugar, etc. When measuring in these fractional cups, level off at the brim.

(c) a graduated set of four spoons: tablespoon *(20 millilitre liquid capacity)*, teaspoon *(5 millilitre)*, half and quarter teaspoons. The Australian, British and American teaspoon each has 5ml capacity.

Approximate cup and spoon conversion chart

Australian	American & British
1 cup	1¼ cups
¾ cup	1 cup
⅔ cup	¾ cup
½ cup	⅔ cup
⅓ cup	½ cup
¼ cup	⅓ cup
2 tablespoons	¼ cup
1 tablespoon	3 teaspoons

All spoon measurements are level.

Note: NZ, USA and UK all use 15ml tablespoons.

We have used large eggs with an average weight of 61g each in all recipes.

All recipes in this book were tested in a 600 watt CONVECTION/MICROWAVE oven

BREAKFASTS BRUNCHES

With a microwave oven your family can fend for themselves at breakfast time. Individual likes and dislikes can be catered for in a flash, e.g., ⅓ cup of old fashioned rolled oats, placed in an individual bowl and topped with ¾ cup hot water, will take 1½ minutes to cook on HIGH — this will give you a bowl of porridge cooked to a creamy consistency. The recipes below will give you some new ideas for breakfast and some tasty dishes for brunch, or even suppers or snacks.

CREAMY EGG AND BACON PIE
PASTRY
1½ cups wholemeal plain flour
125g butter
1 tablespoon water, approximately
FILLING
½ cup grated tasty cheese
4 bacon rashers, finely chopped
1 medium onion, finely chopped
3 eggs
300ml carton cream
½ cup milk
½ teaspoon nutmeg
paprika

Pastry: Sift flour into bowl, rub in butter, mix in enough water to form a dry dough. Knead lightly on floured surface, roll large enough to line pie plate (base measures 18cm). Brush evenly with a little egg white from the Filling, cook on HIGH 6 minutes.

Filling: Sprinkle cheese over pastry case. Combine bacon and onion in bowl, cover with absorbent paper, cook on HIGH 5 minutes, sprinkle over cheese. Beat eggs with cream, milk and nutmeg, pour over bacon mixture. Place pie plate onto an upturned saucer on base plate of microwave oven, cook on MEDIUM 20 minutes or until centre is just set, turn pie halfway through cooking time. Stand 5 minutes, sprinkle with paprika before serving.

ASPARAGUS CHEESE SANDWICH
30g butter
1 teaspoon french mustard
4 slices bread
340g can asparagus spears, drained
¾ cup grated tasty cheese
2 green shallots, chopped
paprika

Combine butter and mustard in dish, cook on HIGH 30 seconds. Brush bread on both sides with mustard butter. Place two slices bread on flat dish, side by side. Place asparagus on top. Top with about ½ cup of the cheese, top with remaining bread. Combine remaining cheese with shallots, sprinkle over bread, sprinkle lightly with paprika. Cook on HIGH 2 minutes or until cheese is melted.
Serves 1 or 2.

CROISSANT HAM AND CHEESE SPLITS
4 croissants
150g sliced ham
1 cup (125g) grated tasty cheese
paprika

Split croissants in half, place cut side up on turntable, top with strips of ham, sprinkle with cheese. Cover with absorbent paper, cook on HIGH 2 minutes or until cheese is just melted. Sprinkle lightly with paprika, serve immediately.
Serves 4.

*Back: Croissant Ham and Cheese Splits;
left: Asparagus Cheese Sandwich;
right: Creamy Egg and Bacon Pie.*

TOASTED HONEY MUESLI

2 cups rolled oats
1 cup unprocessed bran
1 cup shredded coconut
1 cup (185g) slivered almonds
½ cup wheat germ
½ cup sesame seeds
½ cup soybean grits
½ cup skim milk powder
½ cup honey
¼ cup oil
60g unsalted butter
¾ cup (125g) chopped dried
   apricots
¾ cup (125g) chopped pitted
   prunes

Combine first 8 ingredients in large shallow dish. Combine honey, oil and butter in bowl, cook on HIGH 1 minute, stir into dry ingredients. Cook on HIGH 6 minutes, stir well about 3 times during cooking; cool, add apricots and prunes. Store in airtight container in refrigerator.
   Makes about 8 cups.

BANANA CREAM PORRIDGE

1½ cups quick cooking oats
2 cups hot water
½ cup cream
¼ cup brown sugar
2 ripe bananas

Combine porridge and water in large bowl, cook on HIGH 5 minutes. Stir in cream, sugar and one mashed banana. Top with remaining sliced banana and cream, if desired.
   Serves 4.

APRICOTS WITH
CRUMBLE TOPPING

Use your favorite canned fruit for this recipe.

825g can sliced apricots
   in natural fruit syrup
2 tablespoons sunflower
   seed kernels
2 cups bran flakes
¼ cup coconut
¼ cup sultanas
¼ cup honey

Place undrained apricots in four individual dishes. Combine kernels, bran flakes, coconut, sultanas and honey in bowl, cook on HIGH 30 seconds. Sprinkle mixture over apricots, cook on HIGH 4 minutes.
   Serves 4.

CINNAMON GRAPEFRUIT

1 grapefruit
2 teaspoons brown sugar
¼ teaspoon cinnamon

Cut grapefruit in half crossways, segment with grapefruit knife. Sprinkle with combined brown sugar and cinnamon, cook on HIGH 2 minutes, stand before serving.
   Serves 1 or 2.

COCONUT-TOPPED ORANGES

1 orange
2 teaspoons shredded coconut
1 teaspoon golden syrup

Cut orange in half crossways, segment with grapefruit knife. Sprinkle with coconut, drizzle with golden syrup, cook on HIGH 1½ minutes, stand before serving.
   Serves 1 or 2.

MUESLI-TOPPED PEACHES
AND CREAM

825g can peach halves, drained
1 cup toasted muesli
1 tablespoon brown sugar
30g butter
½ cup thickened cream
1 tablespoon honey
¼ teaspoon cinnamon

Place peach halves, cut side up in shallow dish. Combine muesli, brown sugar and chopped butter. Place a tablespoonful of muesli mixture into each peach half. Cook on HIGH 3 minutes. Whip cream until beginning to thicken, beat in honey and cinnamon. Serve with hot peaches.
   Serves 4.

OPPOSITE PAGE: Clockwise from top: Toasted Honey Muesli; Banana Cream Porridge; Apricots with Crumble Topping; Muesli-Topped Peaches and Cream; Coconut-Topped Oranges; Cinnamon Grapefruit.

CORN AND BACON
STUFFED TOMATOES

Choose firm, ripe tomatoes all about the same size; make sure they will sit upright.

4 tomatoes
30g butter
2 green shallots, chopped
1 clove garlic, crushed
2 rashers bacon, chopped
130g can corn kernels, drained
⅓ cup stale breadcrumbs
¼ cup grated tasty cheese

Cut a thick slice from top of each tomato, scoop out pulp carefully with teaspoon, do not break skin of tomato; chop pulp finely. Place butter in bowl, add shallots and garlic, cook on HIGH 1 minute, then add corn, breadcrumbs, cheese and tomato pulp. Place bacon on absorbent paper, cook on HIGH 4 minutes add to corn mixture. Spoon filling into tomatoes, stand tomatoes on plate, cook on HIGH 3 minutes.
   Serves 4.

BELOW: Corn and Bacon Stuffed Tomatoes

CREAMY OMELETTE WITH MUSHROOM SAUCE

4 eggs
¼ cup cream
2 tablespoons orange juice
pinch cayenne pepper
¼ cup grated tasty cheese
MUSHROOM SAUCE
15g butter
2 green shallots, finely chopped
125g mushrooms, roughly chopped
¼ cup sour cream

Beat eggs, cream, orange juice and pepper together with fork. Pour into well greased pie plate, sprinkle with cheese, cook on HIGH 5 minutes. Stand, covered, 3 minutes. Fold in half, serve with Mushroom Sauce.

Mushroom Sauce: Combine butter, shallots and mushrooms in small dish, cook on HIGH 1½ minutes until mushrooms are just soft. Stir in sour cream, cook on HIGH 1 minute.

Serves 2.

FLORENTINE EGGS AND BACON

4 eggs
1 cup cooked spinach
  (see note below)
⅓ cup sour cream
pinch nutmeg
2 teaspoons butter
2 bacon rashers, finely chopped

Puree spinach, sour cream and nutmeg in processor or blender until smooth. Divide mixture between four greased individual dishes. Break an egg into each dish. Place bacon between 2 layers of absorbent paper, cook on HIGH 1½ minutes, sprinkle over egg, dot with butter. Pierce egg yolks in several places with a skewer, cook on HIGH 2 minutes, remove from oven, stand before serving.

Serves 4.

Note: To cook spinach: Place about 4 washed and finely shredded spinach leaves in bowl, cover, cook on HIGH 2 minutes or until wilted. Drain well to remove excess water.

CURRIED SCRAMBLED EGGS

15g butter
1 green shallot, finely chopped
½ teaspoon curry powder
2 eggs
¼ cup milk

Combine butter, shallot and curry powder in pie plate, cook on HIGH 30 seconds. Add combined eggs and milk, cook on HIGH 1 minute, stir outside edges into centre, cook on HIGH further 1 minute. Serve with buttered toast.

Serves 1.

HAM AND EGG MUFFINS
4 English muffins
1 cup (125g) grated tasty cheese
4 eggs
1 teaspoon grainy mustard
30g butter, melted
2 green shallots, chopped
8 slices ham
1 tablespoon chopped fresh dill
   (or ½ teaspoon dried dillweed)
½ cup sour cream
Split muffins in half, scoop out some of the bread from the middle of each muffin to form a cavity, sprinkle each with cheese. Lightly beat eggs with mustard, butter and shallots. Pour over cheese in each muffin, top with a slice of ham. Arrange muffin halves around outside edge of turntable. Cook on HIGH 4 minutes, stand 2 minutes before serving. Serve hot with combined dill and sour cream.
   Serves 4.

PUFFY APPLE CHEESE OMELETTE
2 eggs, separated
1 tablespoon milk
½ teaspoon french mustard
2 tablespoons chopped parsley
2 bacon rashers, chopped
½ Granny Smith apple, coarsely
   grated
¼ cup grated tasty cheese
1 small red pepper, chopped
Beat egg yolks with milk, mustard and parsley, gently fold into firmly beaten egg whites. Place bacon in shallow, round glass dish, (measures 20cm across), cover with absorbent paper. Cook on HIGH 2 minutes. Remove bacon from dish, leave about 2 teaspoons bacon fat in dish. Pour egg mixture into hot bacon fat, sprinkle evenly with apple, cheese and bacon. Cook on MEDIUM-HIGH 2½ minutes, or until just set, sprinkle with red pepper, cover, stand 2 minutes. Fold omelette in half, then serve immediately.
   Serves 2.

Front, from left: Puffy Apple Cheese Omelette; Ham and Egg Muffins.
Back, from left: Creamy Omelette with Mushroom Sauce; Florentine Eggs and Bacon; Curried Scrambled Eggs.

STUFFED MUSHROOMS WITH KIDNEYS

125g lamb's kidneys
4 large flat mushrooms
2 bacon rashers, finely chopped
1 onion, finely chopped
2 teaspoons worcestershire sauce
1 teaspoon soy sauce
2 tablespoons chopped parsley
¼ cup grated tasty cheese

Clean and chop kidneys. Remove stems from mushrooms, chop stems finely; combine with bacon, onion and kidneys; stir in sauces. Cook on HIGH 4 minutes, stir once during cooking time. Stir in half the parsley, place mixture into mushroom caps; top with combined cheese and remaining parsley. Cook on HIGH 4 minutes or until cheese is melted.
  Serves 4.

SAVORY MINCE ON TOAST

30g butter
1 onion, finely chopped
2 medium carrots, finely chopped
750g minced steak
45g packet cream of mushroom
  soup
2 tablespoons tomato sauce
½ teaspoon dried mixed herbs
1½ cups hot water

Combine butter, onion and carrots in shallow dish, cover, cook on HIGH 6 minutes. Add mince, cook on HIGH further 8 minutes until brown, stir meat occasionally during cooking. Add remaining ingredients, cook on HIGH 10 minutes or until meat is tender. Serve on hot toast.
  Serves 4.

SMOKED COD AND CHEESE WITH EGGS

375g smoked cod or haddock
1 small french bread stick
1 cup (125g) grated tasty cheese
1 small red pepper, chopped
2 green shallots, chopped
4 eggs
1 teaspoon french mustard
1 cup milk
1 tablespoon chopped fresh dill
  (or ½ teaspoon dried dillweed)

Place cod in shallow dish, cover with water, cook, covered, on HIGH 4 minutes; stand 5 minutes; drain, remove skin and bones, break fish into chunks. Grease 4 (1 cup fluid capacity) individual dishes. Cut bread into 2.5cm cubes; place a layer of bread cubes in each dish. Top with cod, cheese, pepper and shallots, sprinkle with a few more bread cubes. Beat eggs with fork; add mustard, milk and dill, pour into dishes. Cover, refrigerate overnight. Next day, uncover, cook on HIGH 3 minutes, or until just set. Stand few minutes before serving.
  Serves 4.

SAUSAGES WITH BAKED BEANS

500g (6) thick sausages
1 cup hot water
1 large onion, finely chopped
440g can baby potatoes, drained
440g can baked beans
½ cup grated tasty cheese

Combine sausages and water in shallow dish, cook, covered, on HIGH 6 minutes; drain. Remove skin, cut sausages into 1cm slices. Place onion into dish, cover, cook on HIGH 4 minutes. Layer sausages, sliced potatoes and baked beans on top of onion. Sprinkle with cheese, cook on HIGH 6 minutes.
  Serves 4.

Muffins

Muffins are quick to mix and even quicker to cook. There are a few important things to remember — don't over-mix and don't over-cook muffins, they should be just set, then let stand a few minutes before serving with butter. We used a special microwaveproof six-muffin pan for cooking. However, paper patty cases are fine — we found 4 cases together would support the mixture; arrange them evenly around the outside of the turntable, six at a time. If cooking fewer than six muffins, the cooking time will decrease, e.g., 2 or 3 muffins will take about 45 seconds to cook.

OPPOSITE PAGE:.In descending order: Stuffed Mushrooms with Kidneys; Savory Mince on Toast; Smoked Cod and Cheese with Eggs; Sausages with Baked Beans.

BELOW: Left: Orange and Prune Muffins; in basket, at back: Peanut Butter and Jam Muffins; in basket, in front: Carrot and Walnut Muffins.

ORANGE AND PRUNE MUFFINS

1 medium orange
¼ cup orange juice
60g butter, melted
1 egg
1 cup unprocessed bran
1½ cups self-raising flour
½ cup brown sugar, lightly packed
½ cup chopped pitted prunes
½ cup chopped pecans
¼ cup brown sugar, extra
½ teaspoon cinnamon

Grate, peel and chop orange, combine chopped orange in blender or processor with orange juice, butter and egg, puree until smooth. Sift flour into bowl, add bran, sugar, prunes and orange rind, add orange mixture, stir until just combined. Drop teaspoonfuls of mixture into greased muffin pan. Sprinkle with about one third of the combined pecans, extra sugar and cinnamon. Cook on HIGH 2 minutes. Repeat with remaining mixture.

Makes about 18.

CARROT AND WALNUT MUFFINS

1 cup grated carrot
½ cup sultana bran flakes
1 cup wholemeal self-raising flour
½ teaspoon cinnamon
½ cup brown sugar, lightly packed
¼ cup chopped walnuts
⅔ cup milk
1 egg
60g butter, melted
1 tablespoon lemon juice
walnut halves

Combine carrot, bran flakes, sifted flour, brown sugar, cinnamon and walnuts in bowl. Stir in combined milk, egg, butter and lemon juice, mix until ingredients are just moistened. Drop teaspoonfuls of mixture into greased muffin pan, top with walnut halves if desired, cook on HIGH 2 minutes. Repeat with remaining mixture.

Makes about 18.

PEANUT BUTTER AND JAM MUFFINS

¾ cup self-raising flour
1 cup wheatgerm
⅓ cup brown sugar, firmly packed
1 egg
¼ cup peanut butter
1 tablespoon oil
¾ cup milk
½ cup raspberry jam, approximately
½ cup chopped unsalted roasted peanuts

Combine sifted flour with wheatgerm and sugar in bowl. Blend or process combined egg, peanut butter, oil and milk until smooth. Add to dry ingredients, stir until just combined. Drop teaspoons of mixture into greased muffin pan. Drop a teaspoon of jam onto each muffin, top with another teaspoon of mixture, sprinkle with about one third of the peanuts. Cook on HIGH 2 minutes. Repeat with remaining mixture.

Makes about 12.

SNACKS AND LUNCH DISHES

Here is a selection of light tasty dishes, suitable for lunches or snacks; some of the recipes will appeal particularly to teenagers and children who find microwave ovens fun to use.

NACHOS WITH GUACAMOLE

30g butter
2 large onions, finely chopped
2 cloves garlic, crushed
½ teaspoon chilli powder
1 teaspoon paprika
½ teaspoon dried cumin
400g can tomatoes
2 x 300g cans red kidney beans
100g packet corn chips
1½ cups (200g) grated tasty cheese
GUACAMOLE
1 small ripe avocado
1 small onion, chopped
60g packaged cream cheese
¼ cup plain natural yoghurt
2 teaspoons lemon juice
few drops tabasco sauce

Combine butter, onions, garlic, chilli, paprika and cumin in shallow dish, cook on HIGH 6 minutes or until onions are tender. Drain tomatoes, reserve ¼ cup juice. Drain and rinse beans. Add finely chopped tomatoes and reserved juice to dish with slightly mashed beans, cook on HIGH 10 minutes. Arrange corn chips on large serving dish, sprinkle with 1 cup of the cheese, cook on HIGH 1 minute to melt cheese. Spoon bean mixture into centre of corn chips, top with Guacamole, sprinkle with remaining cheese, cook on HIGH 4 minutes or until cheese is melted.

Guacamole: Peel and seed avocado, puree in blender or processor with remaining ingredients until smooth.

Serves 4 to 6.

CREAMY RED SALMON PATE

30g butter
3 green shallots, chopped
1 tablespoon plain flour
¼ teaspoon dried dill weed
1 teaspoon dry mustard
½ cup sour cream
¼ cup mayonnaise
¼ cup dry white wine
2 tablespoons lemon juice
440g can red salmon
1 tablespoon gelatine
¼ cup water

Combine butter and shallots in bowl, cook on HIGH 3 minutes. Add flour, dill and mustard, cook on HIGH 1 minute, stir in sour cream, mayonnaise, wine and lemon juice. Puree in blender or processor with undrained salmon until smooth. Sprinkle gelatine over water in cup, dissolve by cooking on HIGH for about 20 seconds, cool slightly, stir into salmon mixture. Pour into an oiled 1 litre mould or individual dishes, refrigerate until set. Serve sliced with salad and bread.

Serves 4.

HOT MUSHROOM AND BACON DIP

Make this dish up to 2 days before required, store covered in refrigerator. Reheat on HIGH for about 3 minutes.

4 bacon rashers, finely chopped
15g butter
1 small onion, finely chopped
1 clove garlic, crushed
250g mushrooms, sliced
2 tablespoons plain flour
250g packet cream cheese, chopped
1 teaspoon soy sauce
1 teaspoon worcestershire sauce
1 tablespoon dry sherry
½ cup sour cream

Place bacon in shallow dish, cover with absorbent paper, cook on HIGH 3 minutes or until crisp. Remove bacon from dish, add butter, onion and garlic to dish, cook on HIGH 2 minutes. Stir in mushrooms, cook on HIGH 2 minutes, sprinkle with flour, top with cheese, sauces and sherry, cook on HIGH 5 minutes, stir halfway through cooking time. Stir in sour cream and bacon, spoon into four individual dishes or one larger dish, reheat on HIGH 3 minutes.

Serves 4 as an entree or 8 as a dip.

Clockwise from back right: Golden Sesame Chicken Drumsticks; Ratatouille Lasagna; Crusty Cheese Torpedoes; Hot Mushroom and Bacon Dip; Nachos with Guacamole; Teriyaki Burgers.
Centre left: Creamy Red Salmon Pate; Centre right: Chunky Fried Rice.

TERIYAKI BURGERS

500g minced steak
1 onion, grated
1 egg
1 cup stale breadcrumbs
¼ cup light soy sauce
1 tablespoon honey
1½ tablespoons dry sherry
1 teaspoon grated green ginger
1 clove garlic, crushed
8 hamburger buns, halved
30g butter, melted
2 onions, sliced, extra
2 red peppers, sliced
6 spinach leaves, finely shredded
barbecue or tomato sauce

Combine mince, onion, egg and breadcrumbs in bowl, mix well. Combine soy sauce, honey, sherry, ginger and garlic in bowl, cook on HIGH 2 minutes, add to mince mixture, mix well.

Using well-floured hands, shape mixture into eight hamburger patties, place on large flat dish, cook on HIGH 5 minutes on each side, remove from plate. Place extra onions, peppers and spinach on plate in separate bundles, drizzle with some of the butter, cook on HIGH 3 minutes. Brush inside of buns with remaining butter. Place a burger on each bun, spread with sauce if desired, top with onion, pepper and spinach; replace lid of bun. Heat 4 at a time for 2 minutes on HIGH.

Makes 8.

CRUSTY CHEESE TORPEDOES

250g minced steak
2 crusty french bread sticks
15g butter
4 green shallots, chopped
2 tablespoons gravy powder
1 cup beef stock
¼ cup tomato sauce
1 large tomato, thinly sliced
1 cup grated tasty cheese
1 tablespoon chopped parsley

Halve bread sticks lengthways, scoop out bread from centre, make into breadcrumbs, reserve 1 cup.

Combine butter and shallots in bowl, cook on HIGH 2 minutes, add mince, cook further 4 minutes on HIGH stirring occasionally to break meat up evenly. Stir in gravy powder then stock and tomato sauce, cook on HIGH 6 minutes or until thickened, stir in reserved bread-crumbs. Spoon into bread cases, top with tomato and cheese, cook on HIGH 3 minutes or until cheese is melted. Sprinkle with parsley.

Serves 4.

CHUNKY FRIED RICE

You will need to boil ½ cup rice for this recipe; drain well before using.

4 bacon rashers
2 tablespoons oil
½ teaspoon sesame oil
3 green shallots, chopped
1 clove garlic, crushed
1½ cups cooked long grain rice
1 chicken stock cube
1 teaspoon grated green ginger
2 eggs
125g ham, chopped
250g cooked prawns, shelled
1 tablespoon soy sauce
2 cups shredded lettuce

Place bacon on plate between sheets of absorbent paper, cook on HIGH 4 minutes; crumble bacon when cool. Combine oil, sesame oil, shallots and garlic in large shallow dish. Cook on HIGH 2 minutes, add rice, crumbled stock cube and ginger; cook on HIGH 3 minutes. Beat eggs with fork, pour into greased pie plate, cook on HIGH 2 minutes or until just set; cut into strips. Add ham, bacon, egg, prawns, soy sauce and lettuce to rice mixture, mix well, heat on HIGH 3 minutes, stirring occasionally.

Serves 4

GOLDEN SESAME CHICKEN DRUMSTICKS

8 small chicken drumsticks
90g savory sesame biscuits, crushed
2 teaspoons sesame seeds
½ teaspoon paprika
¼ cup grated parmesan cheese
2 tablespoons chopped parsley
60g butter, melted
1 clove garlic, crushed

Combine biscuits with sesame seeds, paprika, cheese and parsley. Dip chicken in combined butter and garlic, then in sesame mixture. Place around outside of turntable with thickest part of chicken to the outside. Cook on HIGH 10 minutes or until tender.

Serves 4.

RATATOUILLE LASAGNA

4 sheets instant lasagna
1 small eggplant, thinly sliced
salt
1 tablespoon oil
1 onion, chopped
2 cloves garlic, crushed
1 red pepper, chopped
2 tomatoes, peeled, chopped
400g can tomatoes
¼ cup tomato paste
½ teaspoon dried basil leaves
½ teaspoon dried oregano leaves
250g thinly sliced ham
250g mozzarella cheese, sliced
¼ cup grated parmesan cheese

Spread eggplant out onto wire rack, sprinkle with salt on both sides, stand 15 minutes, then pat dry with absorbent paper. Combine oil, onion and garlic in large bowl, cook on HIGH 2 minutes. Chop eggplant finely, add to onion with red pepper, tomatoes, undrained crushed canned tomatoes, tomato paste, basil and oregano. Cook on HIGH 10 minutes. Spread quarter of the eggplant mixture (ratatouille) over base of 20cm square dish, place 2 instant lasagna sheets on top, then another quarter of ratatouille, half the ham, half the mozzarella, then half the parmesan cheese. Repeat with another quarter of ratatouille, two sheets of lasagna, remaining ratatouille, ham, mozzarella and parmesan cheese. Dish must not be more than two thirds full. Cook on HIGH 20 minutes, stand 15 minutes before serving.

Serves 4.

POTATO-TOPPED MINCE PIE

550g minced steak
2 green shallots, chopped
2 teaspoons soy sauce
½ teaspoon dry mustard
1 egg
⅓ cup instant dried potato
⅓ cup tomato sauce
¼ cup chutney
1 tablespoon curry powder
½ cup milk
½ cup instant dried potato, extra
1 cup boiling water
¾ cup milk
30g butter, melted
1 green shallot, chopped, extra

Combine mince with shallots, soy sauce, mustard, egg, tomato sauce, chutney, curry powder, milk and dried potato, mix well. Press firmly into pie plate (base measures 18 cm), cook on HIGH 10 minutes. Combine extra dried potato with remaining ingredients. Spread over mince mixture, reheat on HIGH 2 to 4 minutes.

CREAMY AVOCADO POTATOES

6 medium potatoes
oil
4 bacon rashers, chopped
1 ripe avocado, chopped
125g packet cream cheese
2 tablespoons light sour cream
2 tablespoons chopped chives
1 small red pepper, chopped
caviar

Pierce unpeeled potatoes in several places with fork, rub with oil, place around outside edge of turntable. Cook on HIGH 13 minutes, stand 5 minutes. Cook bacon between sheets of absorbent paper for 3 minutes or until crisp. Cut tops from potatoes, carefully scoop out potato, do not break outside skin of potatoes. Puree potato pulp, avocado, cream cheese and sour cream in blender or processor until smooth. Stir in chives, red pepper and bacon. Spoon potato mixture back into potato shells, cover, cook on HIGH 3 minutes. Top each potato with caviar, if desired.

Serves 4 to 6.

From left: Creamy Avocado Potatoes; Potato-Topped Mince Pie.

MEATBALLS IN TOMATO SAUCE

500g minced steak
1 onion, chopped
½ cup stale breadcrumbs
1 egg
1 clove garlic, crushed
1 teaspoon soy sauce
1 tablespoon chopped parsley
TOMATO SAUCE
1 onion, chopped
400g can tomatoes
1 chicken stock cube
1 tablespoon tomato paste
¼ teaspoon dried oregano leaves
2 teaspoons cornflour
2 teaspoons water

Combine mince, onion, breadcrumbs, egg, garlic and soy sauce in bowl, mix well. Shape mixture into balls, place into Tomato Sauce, cover, cook on HIGH 12 minutes; or until meatballs are tender and cooked through. Sprinkle with parsley.

Tomato Sauce: Combine onion, undrained crushed tomatoes, crumbled stock cube, tomato paste and oregano in shallow dish. Stir in blended cornflour and water.

Serves 4.

BEEF SATAY

It is easier to slice steak thinly if it is partly frozen.

750g rump steak
½ cup peanut butter
¾ cup stock
2 tablespoons dry sherry
1 tablespoon soy sauce
1 tablespoon honey
2 teaspoons curry powder
1 tablespoon oil
2 green shallots, chopped
2 teaspoons cornflour
1 tablespoon water

Cut steak into thin strips. Combine remaining ingredients except cornflour and water, marinate several hours or refrigerate overnight.

Thread steak onto bamboo skewers, place in shallow dish on rack. Cook on HIGH 8 to 10 minutes, turn halfway during cooking time, brush occasionally with marinade. Heat remaining marinade in bowl on HIGH 2 minutes, stir in blended cornflour and water, cook on HIGH 3 minutes or until sauce boils and thickens.

Serve satays on rice, top with sauce.

Makes 12 skewers.

ABOVE: In descending order: Three Cheese Mince and Pasta Casserole; Beef Satay; Meatballs in Tomato Sauce.

OPPOSITE PAGE: From left: Seafood Florentine; Spinach and Salmon Cream; Salmon Croquettes.

THREE CHEESE MINCE AND PASTA CASSEROLE

We used the green spinach-flavored fettucini for this recipe, but any flat egg noodle or pasta can be used. Cooking time will depend on whether the pasta is bought freshly made or pre-packaged.

250g minced steak
250g pork sausage mince
185g fettucini
⅓ cup grated parmesan cheese
1 egg
15g butter
200g ricotta cheese
1 onion, chopped
1 clove garlic, crushed
400g can tomatoes, drained
⅔ cup tomato paste
1 teaspoon sugar
1 teaspoon dried oregano leaves
1 small green pepper, chopped
60g mozzarella cheese, grated

Boil fettucini in large quantity boiling water until just tender; drain, mix in parmesan cheese, egg and butter. Spread into casserole dish, top evenly with crumbled ricotta cheese. Combine minces, onion and garlic in dish, cook on HIGH 6 minutes, stirring twice, drain away excess fat. Add crushed tomatoes, tomato paste, sugar, oregano and pepper. Cook on HIGH 3 minutes, spread over ricotta cheese, sprinkle with mozzarella, cook on HIGH 4 minutes.

Serves 4 to 6.

SEAFOOD FLORENTINE

250g green king prawns
250g scallops
8 spinach leaves, finely shredded
½ cup dry white wine
1 cup milk, approximately
60g butter
2 green shallots, chopped
125g mushrooms, sliced
2 tablespoons plain flour

Place spinach in bowl, cover, cook on HIGH 3 minutes or until just soft. Combine shelled and deveined prawns with scallops and wine in bowl, cover, cook on HIGH 3 minutes or until just tender; drain, reserve stock, make up to 1½ cups with milk. Combine butter, shallots and mushrooms in dish, cook on HIGH 3 minutes or until mushrooms are soft. Stir in flour then stock, cook on HIGH 3 minutes or until thickened. Mix in seafood and spinach, reheat on HIGH 2 minutes if necessary.

Serves 4.

SPINACH AND SALMON CREAM

250g cooked prawns, shelled
250g packet frozen spinach
½ cup thickened cream
1 teaspoon french mustard
220g can salmon, drained
1 tablespoon lemon juice
2 eggs, separated

Thaw spinach on DEFROST for about 9 minutes, drain; press out as much liquid as possible. Puree spinach, cream, mustard, salmon, lemon juice and egg yolks in processor or blender until smooth. Reserve 12 prawns for garnishing, chop remaining prawns, stir into salmon mixture. Beat egg whites until soft peaks form, lightly fold into salmon mixture. Spoon into 4 greased individual dishes (1-cup capacity), cook on MEDIUM HIGH 7 minutes or until mixture is just set in the middle, stand 5 minutes before serving, garnish with reserved prawns.

Serves 4.

SALMON CROQUETTES

440g can salmon, drained
1 onion, finely chopped
2 tablespoons mayonnaise
½ cup grated tasty cheese
⅔ cup instant dried potato
1 cup hot water
125g butter, melted
185g cheese biscuits, crushed
2 tablespoons grated parmesan cheese

Combine salmon, onion, mayonnaise, cheese and dried potato in bowl. Stir in water; mix well. Shape mixture into croquettes. Dip each croquette in butter then roll in combined biscuits and parmesan cheese. Place croquettes on flat dish, cook on HIGH 5 minutes.

Makes 12.

SWEET AND SOUR HAM STEAKS

4 ham steaks
3 tablespoons white vinegar
3 tablespoons sugar
3 tablespoons tomato paste
1½ teaspoons cornflour
1 teaspoon soy sauce
450g can pineapple pieces, drained
1 red pepper, chopped
2 green shallots, chopped

Place ham steaks in shallow dish. Combine vinegar, sugar, tomato paste, cornflour and soy sauce, pour over ham. Add pineapple and pepper, cover, cook on HIGH 7 minutes. Add shallots, cook on HIGH further 1 minute.

Serves 4.

HAM ROLLS WITH BASIL SAUCE

8 slices pressed ham
15g butter
½ teaspoon worcestershire sauce
½ teaspoon dry mustard
4 zucchini, grated
90g mushrooms, finely chopped
5 green shallots, finely chopped
⅓ cup grated parmesan cheese
BASIL SAUCE
15g butter
1 clove garlic, crushed
¼ cup dry white wine
¼ cup finely chopped fresh basil
300ml carton thickened cream
2 egg yolks

Place butter, worcestershire sauce, mustard, zucchini, mushrooms and shallots in bowl, cook on HIGH 5 minutes, stir in cheese. Place a spoonful of mixture onto each slice of ham, roll up, place into a shallow dish. Top with Basil Sauce, cook on MEDIUM HIGH 5 minutes.

Basil Sauce: Combine butter and garlic in bowl, cook on HIGH 30 seconds, add wine, basil and cream, cook on MEDIUM HIGH 5 minutes, stir in egg yolks.

Serves 4.

Back: Ham Rolls with Basil Sauce; Front: Sweet and Sour Ham Steaks.

SOUPS

The full taste and color of soup cooked in a microwave oven are exceptionally good. Remember that there is hardly any evaporation of liquid during the cooking so the flavor of vegetables, herbs, garlic, etc. remains quite strong. Always season to taste after cooking is finished. Where recipes indicate to cover bowl, we used plastic food wrap, placed loosely over the top. In some recipes we have not given a reheating time after pureeing, it is often more practical to reheat the soup in individual serving bowls.

We have used home-made chicken stock in some of our recipes. However, a stock cube and the equivalent amount of water to stock mentioned in the recipes will do instead. A quick, easy, fat-free stock can be made by combining 500g trimmed chicken livers in a large bowl with 6 cups cold water, cover loosely with plastic food wrap, cook on HIGH 30 minutes. Strain livers and discard. Excess stock can be frozen after cooling.

CHUNKY BEEF BORSCH

Best results are from stock made the day before serving so all fat can be removed from the cold stock.

375g beef soup bones
4 cups water
1 bayleaf
1 onion, chopped
1 cup shredded cabbage
1 carrot, sliced
1 medium potato, cubed
3 medium beetroot, peeled, sliced
400g can tomatoes

Combine beef bones, water, bayleaf and onion in large bowl, cover, cook on HIGH until soup boils, then cook further 5 minutes on HIGH. Remove bones, cool, cover, refrigerate, lift off any fat. Add cabbage, carrot, potato, beetroot and undrained crushed tomatoes. Cover, cook on HIGH 15 minutes, discard bayleaf.

Serves 6 to 8.

CURRIED KIWI CLAM SOUP

Mussels can be substituted for kiwi clams in this soup, scrub shells, remove beard. Leave them in the shells when heating. After heating, discard any that do not open.

12 kiwi clams
1 large white fish fillet
   (eg. bream, whiting, etc)
2 cups water
15g butter
2 tablespoons plain flour
2 teaspoons curry powder
2 tablespoons tomato paste
1 chicken stock cube
1 tomato, peeled, chopped
¼ cup cream
2 tablespoons chopped parsley

Cut fish into cubes, place in large bowl with water, cover, cook on HIGH 10 minutes. Drain, reserve stock and fish. Place butter in bowl, cook on HIGH 30 seconds, mix in flour, curry powder, tomato paste and crumbled stock cube. Stir in reserved stock, tomato and fish, cover, cook on HIGH 3 minutes. Add kiwi clams (or mussels), cook on HIGH 2 minutes, stir in cream and parsley before serving.

Serves 4.

CHICKEN AND NOODLE SOUP

1kg chicken pieces
5 cups water
few peppercorns
1 onion, sliced
1 carrot, sliced
½ x 500g packet rice vermicelli
1 carrot, extra
125g mushrooms, sliced
125g bean sprouts
1 tablespoon dry sherry
2 teaspoons soy sauce
2 green shallots, chopped

Combine chicken, water, peppercorns, onion and carrot in large bowl, cover, cook on HIGH 30 minutes. Remove chicken, strain stock; reserve. Place vermicelli in large bowl, cover with water, cook on HIGH 5 minutes; drain. Add vermicelli to stock. Cut extra carrot into thin strips, add to soup, with mushrooms, sprouts, dry sherry and soy sauce. Cover, cook on HIGH 5 minutes. Stir in shallots.

Serves 6 to 8.

From left: Curried Kiwi Clam Soup; Chicken and Noodle Soup; Chunky Beef Borsch.

SOUP IN A PUMPKIN SHELL

Choose pumpkins which will sit level on a plate. If the base is trimmed the soup will escape from the shell. Alternatively, sit pumpkins on a bed of mashed potato when serving.

4 golden nugget pumpkins
2 cups chicken stock
4 tablespoons cream
1 tablespoon chopped chives

Wash pumpkins, cut top from pumpkins, scoop out seeds and pulp from centre, be careful not to break pumpkin shells. Place half a cup of chicken stock into each pumpkin, cover top of pumpkins loosely with plastic wrap, cook on HIGH 10 minutes. Cooking time will depend on size of pumpkins, test from inside for tenderness with fine skewer, do not pierce pumpkin shells. Carefully remove pumpkins from oven, pour liquid into blender or processor, then scoop out soft pumpkin from shells, blend with liquid and cream until smooth. Reheat soup in pumpkin shells or serving bowls on HIGH 2 minutes, sprinkle with chives.

Serves 4.

ZUCCHINI AND LETTUCE SOUP

30g butter
1 onion, sliced
1 clove garlic, crushed
8 (500g) small zucchini, grated
3 lettuce leaves
½ cup chopped parsley
3 cups chicken stock
2 tablespoons grated parmesan cheese

Combine butter, onion and garlic in large bowl, cover, cook on HIGH 3 minutes. Add zucchini, lettuce leaves, parsley and stock, cover, cook on HIGH 12 minutes. Puree in blender or processor, stir in parmesan cheese; reheat.

Serves 4.

BEAN AND TOMATO SOUP

We used chorizo sausage in this soup, but 60g of your favorite salami would be delicious too.

1 tablespoon oil
1 onion, chopped
1 clove garlic, crushed
310g can butter beans (cannellini style)
300g can red kidney beans
400g can tomatoes
2 tablespoons tomato paste
2 cups hot water
¼ teaspoon dried basil leaves
¼ teaspoon dried oregano leaves
1 chorizo sausage, sliced

Combine oil, onion and garlic in large bowl, cover, cook on HIGH 5 minutes add drained and rinsed beans, undrained crushed tomatoes, tomato paste, water, basil and oregano. Cover, cook on HIGH 10 minutes, add sausage.

Serves 4.

TOMATO AND ORANGE SOUP

30g butter
1 onion, chopped
1 clove garlic, crushed
500g medium tomatoes, chopped
1 stick celery, chopped
1 potato, chopped
few strips orange rind
¼ cup orange juice
2 cups chicken stock
2 tablespoons chopped fresh basil or 1 teaspoon dried basil leaves

Combine butter, onion and garlic in bowl, cover, cook on HIGH 3 minutes. Add tomatoes, celery, potato, orange rind, orange juice and chicken stock, cover, cook on HIGH 20 minutes. Remove rind, puree soup in blender or processor with basil; reheat before serving.

Serves 4.

Above: Zucchini and Lettuce Soup; Below: Soup in a Pumpkin Shell.

CORN AND PUMPKIN SOUP

1 butternut pumpkin (about 1kg), peeled, diced
2 onions, chopped
60g butter
3½ cups chicken stock
440g can creamed corn
3 teaspoons worcestershire sauce
½ cup cream
1 tablespoon chopped chives

Combine pumpkin, onions and butter in large bowl, cover, cook on HIGH 3 minutes. Add chicken stock, cover, cook on HIGH 25 minutes. Puree in blender or processor, stir in corn, worcestershire sauce and cream, reheat, sprinkle with chives.

Serves 6.

CURRIED PEA SOUP

100g packet dehydrated peas
1 teaspoon sugar
4 cups chicken stock
1 cup milk
15g butter
2 teaspoons curry powder

Combine peas, sugar and stock in large bowl, cover, cook on HIGH 20 minutes. Drain peas, reserve stock. Puree peas in blender or processor with milk. Place butter and curry powder in bowl, cook on HIGH 1 minute, add pea puree and reserved stock, cook on HIGH 2 minutes.

Serves 4.

Clockwise from bottom: Corn and Pumpkin Soup; Bean and Tomato Soup; Tomato and Orange Soup; Creamy Mushroom Soup; Curried Pea Soup.

CREAMY MUSHROOM SOUP

60g butter
250g mushrooms, chopped
2 cups chicken stock
¼ cup dry white wine
1 teaspoon french mustard
½ cup cream
1 tablespoon chopped chives

Combine butter and mushrooms in large bowl, cover, cook on HIGH 4 minutes, mix in stock, wine, mustard and cream, cover, cook on HIGH 10 minutes. Puree in blender or processor, stir in chives; reheat.

Serves 4.

SEAFOOD

Seafood of all types cooks superbly in a microwave oven. When cooking fish fillets, cutlets or steaks, try to buy them all the same size for even cooking results. Any type of fish can be used. We chose white fish fillets; bream, flathead, snapper, jewfish, whiting, etc., are all ideal. We've included quite a lot of salmon recipes; tuna can be substituted if preferred. Be careful not to overcook prawns, scallops and squid. As with conventional methods, overcooking means rubbery seafood. When food requires covering in recipes, simply cover loosely with plastic food wrap. Be careful of steam when removing the wrap. Oysters and mussels can be opened in the oven. They will take between 30 seconds and two minutes, depending on size. Remove them from the oven as they open; overcooking will make them tough. Discard any that do not open after 2 minutes.

FISH WITH PINEAPPLE AND GINGER

4 white fish fillets
1 small carrot
½ small onion, chopped
1 small stick celery, chopped
½ cup (60g) roasted unsalted cashews
2 teaspoons grated green ginger
2 teaspoons butter
½ x 450g can crushed pineapple, drained
1 small red pepper, chopped
¼ cup stale wholemeal breadcrumbs
½ cup thickened cream
2 teaspoons soy sauce
4 green shallots, chopped

Remove skin and bones from fish. Chop carrot into fine strips, combine in bowl with onion, celery, cashews, ginger and butter, cook on HIGH 3 minutes. Stir in pineapple, pepper and breadcrumbs. Divide filling evenly over fish, fold fish over to enclose filling, secure with toothpicks. Place fish into a greased dish, the fold in the fish should be toward the outside edge of dish. Pour over combined cream and soy sauce, cover, cook on HIGH 7 minutes, or until fish is tender, sprinkle with shallots.

Serves 4.

SEAFOOD AND BACON KEBABS

We flavored and colored the rice with a tiny pinch of saffron during the cooking.

500g green king prawns
250g scallops
5 bacon rashers
2 tablespoons lemon juice
30g butter
1 onion, finely chopped
1 clove garlic, crushed
2 teaspoons cornflour
1 tablespoon dry sherry
1 cup chicken stock
¼ cup cream

Shell and devein prawns, clean scallops. Cut bacon rashers crosswise into 3, roll each piece tightly, thread onto 8 bamboo skewers alternating with prawns and scallops, brush with lemon juice. Combine butter, onion and garlic in shallow dish, cook on HIGH 3 minutes. Add kebabs to dish, brush with onion butter, cook on HIGH 4 minutes or until seafood is cooked, turn once during cooking. Remove kebabs to serving plate, stir cornflour into butter, cook on HIGH 1 minute. Stir in sherry, stock and cream, cook on HIGH 3 minutes or until sauce boils and thickens. Serve kebabs with rice, topped with sauce.

Serves 4.

Clockwise from centre front: Fish with Lemon Butter Sauce; Tomatoes with Crab and Camembert; Garlic Prawns; Fish with Pineapple and Ginger; Seafood and Bacon Kebabs; Seafood in Creamy Tomato Sauce; Sweet and Sour Fish Cocktails.

SEAFOOD IN CREAMY TOMATO SAUCE

500g green king prawns
1 squid
15g butter
1 clove garlic, crushed
2 tomatoes, peeled, chopped
1 tablespoon tomato paste
¼ cup dry white wine
2 teaspoons chopped fresh basil
¼ cup cream

Peel prawns, leave tails intact, remove back veins, split prawns in half lengthways. Clean squid, slice into rings. Place seafood into dish. Combine butter and garlic in bowl, cook on HIGH 1 minute, stir in tomatoes, tomato paste and wine, cook on HIGH 5 minutes. Puree in blender or processor with basil and cream, strain, pour over seafood, cook on HIGH 5 minutes or until prawns are tender. Serve with pasta or rice.

Serves 4.

FISH WITH LEMON BUTTER SAUCE

4 white fish fillets
4 spinach leaves, shredded
2 small zucchini, sliced
1 small red pepper, sliced
1 stick celery, sliced
LEMON BUTTER SAUCE
1 tablespoon water
1 tablespoon white vinegar
185g butter
1 teaspoon grated lemon rind
2 green shallots, chopped

Combine spinach and zucchini in shallow dish, cover, cook on HIGH 1 minute. Add pepper and celery to spinach. Place fish on top, cover, cook on HIGH 5 minutes, top with Lemon Butter Sauce.

Lemon Butter Sauce: Combine water, vinegar and one-third of the butter in dish, cook on HIGH 1 minute. Cut remaining cold butter into small cubes, gradually whisk into Sauce until thick, stir in lemon rind and shallots.

Serves 4.

SWEET AND SOUR FISH COCKTAILS

Buy cold, pre-cooked fish cocktails from your local fish shop.

500g fish cocktails or fish pieces
1 red pepper, chopped
1 onion, chopped
3 green shallots, chopped
SAUCE
1 cup hot water
½ cup sugar
½ cup white vinegar
1 tablespoon cornflour
1 tablespoon soy sauce

Combine pepper and onion in shallow bowl, cover, cook on HIGH 2 minutes. Add fish and Sauce, cover, cook on HIGH 5 minutes. Add shallots, cook on HIGH 1 minute.

Sauce: Combine water and sugar in bowl, stir until sugar is dissolved. Stir in cornflour blended with vinegar and soy sauce. Cook on HIGH 2 minutes or until Sauce boils and thickens, stir after 1 minute.

Serves 4.

TOMATOES WITH CRAB AND CAMEMBERT

Cook ¼ cup pastina (rice-shaped pasta) or rice for this recipe.

6 medium tomatoes
125g packet camembert cheese
180g can crab, drained
1 tablespoon sour cream
1 tablespoon lemon juice
2 green shallots, chopped
1 teaspoon capers, chopped
¾ cup cooked pastina
2 tablespoons chopped parsley

Cut a thick slice from top of each tomato. Scoop out pulp with teaspoon; reserve for another use. Remove rind from cheese, chop cheese finely; place in bowl, mix in crab, sour cream, lemon juice, shallots, capers, pastina and parsley. Spoon mixture into tomato shells, place in shallow dish, cook on HIGH 5 minutes.

Serves 6.

GARLIC PRAWNS

1kg green king prawns
1 cup oil
125g butter
8 cloves garlic, crushed
2 small red chillies, finely chopped
1 tablespoon chopped parsley
1 tablespoon lemon juice

Shell prawns, leave tail intact, remove back vein. Divide oil, butter, garlic and chillies evenly between 4 individual dishes. Cook on HIGH 4 minutes, or until oil is bubbling. Add prawns, cook on HIGH further 1 to 2 minutes, or until prawns turn pink. Serve immediately, sprinkled with parsley and lemon juice.

Serves 4.

CRAB AND SPINACH WITH PASTA
CHEESE SAUCE
250g spiral pasta, cooked
30g butter
2 tablespoons plain flour
¼ cup dry white wine
300ml carton thickened cream
90g swiss cheese, grated
paprika
CRAB FILLING
1 clove garlic, crushed
250g mushrooms, sliced
15g butter
6 spinach leaves, chopped
1 tablespoon lemon juice
185g can crab meat, drained

Cheese Sauce: Melt butter in bowl on HIGH 1 minute, stir in flour, then wine and cream, cook on HIGH 3 minutes, or until sauce boils and thickens; add cheese, stir until melted. Stir half the Cheese Sauce into pasta, place into dish, top with Filling, then remaining Cheese Sauce. Sprinkle with paprika, cook on HIGH 5 minutes, or until heated through.

Crab Filling: Cook garlic, mushrooms and butter in bowl on HIGH 3 minutes, add spinach, lemon juice and crab, cook, covered, on HIGH 3 minutes or until spinach is wilted.

Serves 4.

CRAB AND WINE MORNAY
60g butter
¼ cup plain flour
2 teaspoons french mustard
½ cup milk
½ cup cream
⅓ cup dry white wine
60g mozzarella cheese, grated
1 tablespoon grated parmesan cheese
4 green shallots, chopped
1 tablespoon chopped parsley
2 x 200g cans crab, drained
TOPPING
⅓ cup packaged breadcrumbs
1 teaspoon paprika
1 tablespoon chopped parsley
60g mozzarella cheese, grated
2 tablespoons grated parmesan cheese

Put butter in dish, cook on HIGH 1 minute, add flour and mustard, cook on HIGH 1 minute. Gradually stir in milk, cream and wine, stir until smooth, cook on HIGH 3 minutes or until mixture boils and thickens. Stir in mozzarella and parmesan cheese, shallots, parsley and crab. Spoon into four individual dishes, sprinkle with Topping, cover, cook on HIGH 2 minutes or until cheese is melted.

Topping: Combine all ingredients.
Serves 4.

Back: Crab and Spinach with Pasta;
Front: Crab and Wine Mornay.

SALMON IN CABBAGE ROLLS

You will need to cook about 1 cup rice for this recipe.

8 whole cabbage leaves
440g can salmon, drained
2 medium carrots, finely grated
2½ cups cooked rice
¼ cup mayonnaise
2 cups chicken stock
¼ cup tomato paste
½ teaspoon dried basil leaves
2 tablespoons plain flour
2 tablespoons water

Remove any thick stalk from cabbage leaves. Place leaves into large shallow dish, cover, cook on HIGH 5 minutes, drain. Mix salmon with carrot, rice and mayonnaise. Divide mixture into 6 portions, spoon onto cabbage leaves, roll up tightly, tucking in ends. Place into shallow dish in single layer. Combine stock, tomato paste and basil, pour over rolls, cover, cook on HIGH 15 minutes or until tender. Remove rolls, keep warm. Blend flour with a little water, stir into liquid in dish, cook on HIGH 3 minutes or until mixture boils and thickens, serve over rolls.

Serves 4.

SPINACH AND SALMON LOAF

9 spinach leaves
2 x 220g cans salmon, drained
3 eggs
½ cup milk
1 tablespoon lemon juice
⅓ cup stale breadcrumbs
2 tablespoons grated parmesan cheese

Front: Spinach and Salmon Loaf; Back left: Salmon in Cabbage Rolls; Right: High Fibre Salmon and Vegetable Casserole.

HIGH FIBRE SALMON AND VEGETABLE CASSEROLE

Cook about ⅔ cup brown rice for this recipe; drain well before using.

15g butter
1 onion, chopped
1 carrot, chopped
1 stick celery, chopped
1½ cups cooked brown rice
1 egg
1 tablespoon tomato paste
90g mushrooms, sliced
1 small red pepper, chopped
220g can salmon
130g can whole kernel corn, drained
1 tablespoon chopped chives
½ cup grated tasty cheese

Combine butter, onion, carrot and celery in dish, cover, cook on HIGH 5 minutes; add rice, lightly beaten egg, tomato paste, mushrooms, red pepper, undrained salmon, corn and chives, mix until well combined. Sprinkle with cheese, cook on HIGH 8 minutes.
Serves 4.

SAUCY FISH WITH MUSHROOMS

6 white fish fillets
15g butter
1 onion, chopped
1 clove garlic, crushed
3 tomatoes, peeled, chopped
125g mushrooms, sliced
2 tablespoons dry white wine
¼ teaspoon dried basil leaves
¼ cup mayonnaise
1 teaspoon grated lemon rind
3 green shallots, chopped
2 teaspoons cornflour
1 tablespoon dry white wine, extra

Remove skin and bones from fish. Cook butter, onion and garlic in bowl on HIGH 3 minutes. Add tomatoes, mushrooms, wine and basil, cook on HIGH 4 minutes. Combine mayonnaise, lemon rind and shallots, spread over skin side of each fish fillet. Roll fillets, place in shallow dish seam side down, in single layer. Top with tomato mixture, cover, cook on HIGH 7 minutes or until fish is just tender. Remove fish from dish, keep warm. Stir blended cornflour and extra wine into pan, cook on HIGH 5 minutes, or until mixture boils and thickens, stir once during cooking. Serve sauce over fish.
Serves 6.

CAMEMBERT FISH IN PARSLEY SAUCE

125g packet camembert cheese
4 large white fish fillets
¼ cup dry white wine
⅔ cup milk, approximately
30g butter
1 tablespoon plain flour
2 teaspoons chopped parsley

Remove skin and bones from fish. Split camembert through centre, open out to form two complete rounds, cut each round in half to give four semi-circles. Cut each fish fillet in half crossways. Place the tail end of fillets in shallow dish, in single layer. Top each with a piece of camembert, cover with remaining fish pieces. Pour wine over, cover, cook on HIGH 5 minutes or until just cooked. Remove fish, cover, keep warm. Measure liquid in dish, make up to 1 cup with milk. Melt butter in dish on HIGH 30 seconds, add flour, cook on HIGH 1 minute, stir in the milk mixture and parsley. Cook on HIGH 3 minutes or until sauce boils and thickens. Pour sauce over fish, serve immediately.
Serves 4.

HERBED FISH IN AN OVEN BAG

Be careful of steam when opening oven bag.

4 fish cutlets or steaks
30g butter
1 onion, sliced
2 tomatoes, peeled, sliced
1 green pepper, sliced
2 tablespoons lemon juice
¼ cup dry white wine
1 teaspoon dried tarragon leaves
1 tablespoon chopped chives
3 teaspoons cornflour
2 tablespoons water

Combine butter, onion, tomatoes and pepper in oven bag, twist end, tuck end underneath. Cook on HIGH 5 minutes. Place fish on top of vegetables in bag, sprinkle with lemon juice, wine, tarragon and chives, twist end, tuck underneath; cook on HIGH 5 minutes. Pour juices carefully into small bowl, (leave fish, etc, in bag to keep warm), stir in blended cornflour and water, cook on HIGH 2 minutes, or until sauce boils and thickens. Place fish and vegetables on plate, top with sauce.
Serves 4.

Rinse spinach under water; cut away stalks. Place spinach in bowl, cover, cook on HIGH 1 minute. Line a lightly greased ovenproof dish (base measures 9cm x 22cm) with 3 or 4 of the spinach leaves, leaving spinach overlapping sides. Chop remaining spinach, squeeze out excess moisture. Combine eggs, milk, salmon, lemon juice, breadcrumbs and cheese, stir in spinach. Spoon mixture into spinach-lined dish, enclose filling by overlapping spinach leaves, cover, cook on HIGH 13 minutes, stand 5 minutes before turning out. Serve hot or cold.
Serves 4 to 6.

FISH WITH GRATED VEGETABLE TOPPING

4 white fish fillets
2 tablespoons lemon juice
2 small carrots, coarsely grated
2 zucchini, coarsely grated
2 bacon rashers, chopped
2 green shallots, chopped
2 teaspoons soy sauce

Remove bones and skin from fish, place in single layer in shallow dish, sprinkle with lemon juice. Combine carrots, zucchini, bacon, shallots and soy sauce, mix well, press firmly onto fish, cook on HIGH 10 minutes or until fish is tender.

Serves 4.

LEFT: In descending order: Fish with Spinach and Mushrooms; Saucy Fish with Mushrooms; Camembert Fish in Parsley Sauce; Creamy Seafood Slice; Herbed Fish in an Oven Bag.

CREAMY SEAFOOD SLICE

4 white fish fillets
2 tablespoons lemon juice
440g can salmon, drained
300ml carton sour cream
3 eggs
½ cup grated tasty cheese
2 tablespoons mayonnaise
2 green shallots, chopped

Remove skin and bones from fish. Place fish in shallow dish, sprinkle with lemon juice, cover, cook on HIGH 4 minutes or until just cooked; drain well. Mash salmon with a fork, press over fish to give a firm, even layer. Beat sour cream, eggs, cheese, mayonnaise and shallots lightly with a fork, pour over salmon, cover, cook on DEFROST 15 to 20 minutes or until just set. Stand 5 minutes before cutting or serve cold.

Serves 4 to 6.

FISH WITH SPINACH AND MUSHROOMS

500g white fish fillets
90g mushrooms, sliced
15g butter
250g packet frozen spinach
1 onion, chopped
440g can cream of mushroom soup
⅓ cup grated tasty cheese

Remove skin and bones from fish, cut into chunks place in single layer in 4 individual dishes. Top with mushrooms, dot with butter. Place spinach and onion in bowl, cook on HIGH 3 minutes or until spinach is thawed. Stir in undiluted soup, pour over fish, sprinkle with cheese, cook on HIGH 10 minutes.

Serves 4.

FISH WITH LEMON SAUCE

4 white fish fillets
1 lemon
2 teaspoons dry sherry
1 red pepper
LEMON SAUCE
3 teaspoons cornflour
¼ cup lemon juice
1 teaspoon soy sauce
1 teaspoon tomato sauce
1½ tablespoons sugar
½ cup water.

Remove skin and bones from fish; place fish in single layer in shallow dish. Cut two strips from lemon using vegetable peeler; shred lemon rind finely. Cut pepper into thin strips. Sprinkle sherry over fish, cook on HIGH 6 minutes. Sprinkle pepper strips and lemon rind over fish, pour Sauce over, cook on HIGH 1 minute, or until heated through.

Lemon Sauce: Blend cornflour with lemon juice in bowl add remaining ingredients, cook on HIGH 2 minutes, stirring after 1 minute. Serves 4.

POTATO-TOPPED SMOKED FISH CASSEROLE

500g smoked cod or haddock
1 cup water
30g butter
2 teaspoons french mustard
2 tablespoons plain flour
1¼ cups milk
½ teaspoon dried tarragon leaves
2 green shallots, chopped
POTATO TOPPING
500g potatoes, chopped
2 tablespoons water
30g butter
⅓ cup milk
1 tablespoon chopped parsley
½ cup grated tasty cheese

Front: Fish with Lemon Sauce; Back row, left: Fish with Grated Vegetable Topping; Right: Potato-Topped Smoked Fish Casserole.

Place cod and water in bowl, cover, cook on HIGH 7 minutes, stand 5 minutes; drain and flake fish. Combine butter, mustard and flour in bowl, cook on HIGH 1 minute, stir in milk and tarragon, cook on HIGH 5 minutes, stirring occasionally. Stir in fish and shallots. Pipe or spread Potato Topping around edge of dish, cook on HIGH 4 minutes, or until heated through.

Potato Topping: Combine potatoes and water in bowl, cook, covered, on HIGH 9 minutes or until tender, drain. Mash potatoes, add butter, milk, parsley and cheese, beat well.

Serves 4.

CHICKEN

Chicken is beautifully moist and tender cooked in a microwave oven; be careful not to over-cook. Standing time allows for extra cooking in some recipes. Cover food loosely with plastic wrap when recipe specifies. Remove as much fat as possible before cooking chicken — remove skin where indicated in recipes.

CHICKEN WITH SWEET APPLE AND RAISIN SEASONING
No. 15 chicken
1 tablespoon soy sauce
¼ cup red currant jelly
2 tablespoons barbecue sauce
1 tablespoon brandy
1 tablespoon plain flour
12 small onions, peeled
APPLE RAISIN SEASONING
2 cups stale breadcrumbs
4 green shallots, chopped
1 clove garlic, crushed
30g butter
1 small stick celery, chopped
⅓ cup chopped dried apples
1 tablespoon chopped raisins
2 tablespoons chopped parsley
1 egg

Rub skin of chicken all over with soy sauce. Fill chicken cavity with Seasoning, secure opening with skewer. Combine red currant jelly, barbecue sauce and brandy in bowl, cook on HIGH 1 minute, brush chicken with this sauce. Coat inside of a large (turkey-sized) oven bag with flour, shake away excess flour. Place chicken in bag with onions, pour over remaining sauce. Cut off 2.5cm strip across top of oven bag, tie oven bag with strip, place bag in shallow dish, cook on HIGH 25 minutes. Stand 10 minutes before serving.

Apple Raisin Seasoning; Combine shallots, garlic, butter and celery in small bowl, cook on HIGH 1 minute, mix into breadcrumbs. Combine apples and raisins in dish, cover with water, cook on HIGH 2 minutes, drain well, add to breadcrumb mixture with parsley and egg.
Serves 4 to 6.

BARBECUED CHICKEN IN PROVENCALE SAUCE
1 barbecued chicken
1 onion, finely chopped
1 clove garlic, crushed
2 teaspoons oil
125g mushrooms, sliced
2 x 400g cans tomatoes
2 tablespoons tomato paste
2 tablespoons dry white wine
½ teaspoon dried basil leaves
1 small green pepper, chopped
8 whole black olives
2 tablespoons chopped parsley

Cut chicken into serving-sized pieces. Combine onion, garlic and oil in large shallow dish, cook on HIGH 3 minutes. Add mushrooms, undrained crushed tomatoes, tomato paste, wine, basil and chicken, cook on HIGH 4 minutes, stir in pepper and olives, cook on HIGH 2 minutes, sprinkle with parsley before serving.
Serves 4.

TOMATO MOZZARELLA CHICKEN
4 chicken breast fillets
1 cup cornflakes, crushed
⅓ cup grated parmesan cheese
2 tablespoons chopped parsley
1 egg
310g can Tomato Supreme
4 slices mozzarella cheese

Combine cornflakes with cheese and parsley. Dip chicken fillets into beaten egg, then coat in cornflake mixture. Place into shallow dish in single layer, cook on HIGH 10 minutes, or until just tender. Top each fillet with a spoonful of Tomato Supreme and 1 slice of mozzarella. Cook on HIGH 2 minutes or until cheese has melted.
Serves 4.

TURMERIC CHICKEN WITH CORN
4 chicken breast fillets
½ teaspoon turmeric
2 teaspoons grated green ginger
1 tablespoon soy sauce
1 red pepper
1 green pepper
1 teaspoon cornflour
2 tablespoons water
425g can young corn, drained

Cut chicken fillets into 1cm strips, combine with turmeric, ginger and soy sauce, mix well, stand 15 minutes. Cut peppers into strips. Place chicken in shallow dish, cook on HIGH 3 minutes. Add blended cornflour and water, peppers and corn, cook on HIGH 4 minutes, or until mixture boils and thickens, stir once during cooking.
Serves 4.

Clockwise from front: Ham and Chicken Rolls; Chicken Maryland Supreme; Chicken with Sweet Apple and Raisin Seasoning; Barbecued Chicken in Provencale Sauce; Turmeric Chicken with Corn; Chicken in Peanut Sauce. Centre: Tomato Mozzarella Chicken.

HAM AND CHICKEN ROLLS

8 chicken thigh fillets
100g ham
4 flat mushrooms
4 green shallots
1½ tablespoons hoisin sauce
1 tablespoon soy sauce
¼ teaspoon sesame oil
2 teaspoons sesame seeds

Cut ham, mushrooms and shallots into long thin strips. Combine sauces and sesame oil; brush each side of each fillet with some of this sauce mixture, place ham, mushroom and shallot strips along centre of each fillet, roll up, secure with toothpick, place around outside edge of turntable. Brush with remaining sauce mixture, sprinkle with sesame seeds, cook on HIGH 10 minutes.

Serves 4.

CHICKEN MARYLAND SUPREME

4 chicken marylands
2 bacon rashers, chopped
1 onion, chopped
1½ cups stale breadcrumbs
2 green shallots, chopped
2 teaspoons french mustard
1 egg
440g can new potatoes, drained, sliced
310g can Tomato Supreme
2 teaspoons worcestershire sauce

Combine bacon and onion in small bowl, cook on HIGH 2 minutes, mix in breadcrumbs, shallots, mustard and lightly beaten egg. Loosen skin on chicken with fingers. Push stuffing gently under skin down to the drumstick. Place chicken in shallow dish in single layer, cook on HIGH 8 minutes. Add potatoes, top with combined Tomato Supreme and worcestershire sauce, cook on HIGH 8 minutes, or until chicken is tender, baste once during cooking.

Serves 4.

CHICKEN IN PEANUT SAUCE

8 chicken thigh fillets
1 onion, finely chopped
1 clove garlic, crushed
30g butter
¼ cup crunchy peanut butter
½ cup chicken stock
¼ cup honey
2 teaspoons grainy mustard
1 teaspoon curry powder
pinch cardamom
dash tabasco sauce

Remove any fat and sinew from chicken. Combine onion, garlic and butter in dish, cook on HIGH 3 minutes. Stir in peanut butter, stock, honey, mustard, curry, cardamom and tabasco, add chicken in single layer. Cook on HIGH 6 minutes, turn chicken, cook on HIGH 6 minutes. Serve with rice.

Serves 4.

CREAMY CHICKEN MARSALA

4 chicken breast fillets
4 zucchini, sliced
2 tomatoes, peeled, chopped
2 cloves garlic, crushed
¼ teaspoon dried oregano
½ cup chicken stock
⅓ cup marsala
¼ cup plain flour
⅓ cup chicken stock, extra
¼ cup cream
4 green shallots, chopped

Cut chicken into bite-sized pieces, combine with zucchini, tomatoes, garlic, oregano, stock and marsala in shallow dish. Cook on HIGH 10 minutes or until chicken is tender, stirring occasionally. Blend flour with extra stock, stir into mixture with cream and shallots. Cook on HIGH 5 minutes or until mixture boils and thickens. Serve with rice, if desired.

Serves 4.

ALL-IN-ONE CHICKEN CASSEROLE

4 chicken breast fillets
2 large potatoes, thinly sliced
2 teaspoons grated green ginger
2 tablespoons dry sherry
1 tablespoon soy sauce
1 teaspoon sugar
2 tablespoons cornflour
1 cup chicken stock
185g mushrooms, sliced
4 green shallots, chopped

Chop chicken into bite-sized pieces, combine with potatoes, ginger, sherry, soy sauce and sugar. Stir in blended cornflour and stock, cook on HIGH 20 minutes or until potatoes are tender, stirring occasionally. Add mushrooms and shallots, cook on HIGH 10 minutes.

Serves 4.

CHICKEN IN MANGO SAUCE

4 chicken breast fillets
1 mango
30g butter
1 onion, finely chopped
1 teaspoon grated lemon rind
1 tablespoon lemon juice
1 chicken stock cube
1 tablespoon cornflour
⅓ cup water
1 stick celery, finely chopped
2 tablespoons chopped walnuts
¼ cup sour cream

Puree mango pulp in blender or processor. Combine butter and onion in dish, cook on HIGH 3 minutes. Add mango, lemon rind, lemon juice and crumbled stock cube, stir in blended cornflour and water, cook on HIGH 1 minute, stir; cook further 1 minute. Stir in celery, walnuts and sour cream. Place chicken in single layer in shallow dish, cover with sauce, cook on HIGH 3 minutes, turn chicken, cook on HIGH 6 minutes.

Serves 4.

CHICKEN AND BACON WITH CORN SAUCE

6 chicken breast fillets
300g can creamed corn
1 green shallot, finely chopped
1 bacon rasher, chopped
¼ cup chicken stock
2 tablespoons cream
1 teaspoon french mustard
⅓ cup grated tasty cheese
1 tablespoon chopped parsley

Cut a deep pocket in thickest part of each fillet. Mix together ¼ of the creamed corn, shallot and bacon. Place a teaspoonful of corn mixture into pocket of each fillet. Place chicken in single layer in shallow dish, pour stock over chicken, cook on HIGH 6 minutes. Drain liquid from dish, combine it with remaining corn, cream and mustard, blend or process corn mixture until smooth, pour over chicken, sprinkle with cheese, cook on HIGH 6 minutes. Serve sprinkled with parsley.

Serves 4 to 6.

In descending order; All-in-One Chicken Casserole; Chicken in Mango Sauce; Creamy Chicken Marsala; Chicken and Bacon with Corn Sauce.

SPICY MARINATED CHICKEN

4 chicken breast fillets
2 cloves garlic, crushed
3 tablespoons lemon juice
1 teaspoon ground ginger
1 teaspoon turmeric
½ teaspoon nutmeg
1 teaspoon ground coriander
½ teaspoon paprika
¼ teaspoon cayenne pepper
1 teaspoon garam masala
½ teaspoon cinnamon
pinch saffron powder
½ cup sour cream

Marinate chicken fillets in combined garlic, lemon juice, ginger, turmeric, nutmeg, coriander, paprika, cayenne pepper, garam masala, cinnamon and saffron powder for several hours or refrigerated overnight.

Place chicken fillets in dish in single layer, cover, cook on HIGH 12 minutes. Pour sour cream over chicken, cook on HIGH 1 minute.

Serves 4.

CHUNKY CHICKEN WITH MUSHROOMS

Size 15 chicken
1 clove garlic, crushed
15g butter
1 onion, finely chopped
125g mushrooms, sliced
1 small red pepper, sliced
2 sticks celery, sliced
1 tablespoon plain flour
2 tablespoons water
½ teaspoon paprika
1 tablespoon dry sherry
2 egg yolks
¼ cup cream
1 chicken stock cube

Cook garlic and butter in shallow dish on HIGH 2 minutes. Place chicken in dish, brush chicken with garlic butter, cover with absorbent paper, cook on HIGH 12 minutes; turn chicken, brush with pan drippings, cover with absorbent paper, cook on HIGH further 12 minutes. Remove chicken from pan, wrap in aluminium foil, stand 20 minutes while preparing vegetable mixture.

Place onion, mushrooms, pepper and celery into dish with pan drippings, cook on HIGH 5 minutes. Blend flour with water, add paprika, sherry, egg yolks, cream and crumbled stock cube. Stir into vegetable mixture, cook on HIGH 2 minutes. Remove chicken from foil, reserve ¼ cup of juices from foil. Remove skin and bones from chicken, cut chicken into chunky pieces. Stir reserved juices into vegetables with chicken pieces, cover, cook on HIGH 3 minutes, stir once. Serve with rice or noodles.

Serves 4 to 6.

LEFT: Back: Chunky Chicken with Mushrooms; Front: Spicy Marinated Chicken.

OPPOSITE PAGE: Back: Chicken, Leek and Pasta Casserole; Left: Chicken in Tangy Tomato Sauce; Right: Cold Chicken in Pimiento Sauce.

CHICKEN, LEEK AND PASTA CASSEROLE

Cook 2 cups pasta for this recipe. We used the spiral shaped variety.

1 barbecued chicken
4 cups cooked pasta
60g butter
⅓ cup plain flour
1½ cups milk
½ cup dry white wine
1 cup grated tasty cheese
¼ cup grated parmesan cheese
4 leeks, sliced
30g butter, extra
½ cup grated tasty cheese, extra
¼ cup grated parmesan cheese, extra

Remove skin and bones from chicken, cut chicken into chunks. Place butter in bowl, melt on HIGH 1 minute. Stir in flour, then milk and wine, cook on HIGH 5 minutes, or until sauce boils and thickens, stirring once; add cheeses, stir until melted. Stir 1 cup of sauce into cooked pasta, add remaining sauce to chicken. Put extra butter in dish, melt on HIGH 30 seconds, add leeks, cook on HIGH 5 minutes. Place chicken in dish, top with leek mixture, then pasta. Sprinkle with extra combined cheeses, cook on HIGH 5 minutes or until hot.
Serves 4.

CHICKEN IN TANGY TOMATO SAUCE

1kg chicken pieces
1 onion, finely chopped
1 stick celery, chopped
4 medium ripe tomatoes, peeled, chopped
1 tablespoon cornflour
2 tablespoons vinegar
1 clove garlic, crushed
¼ cup tomato sauce
1 tablespoon worcestershire sauce
½ cup water
1 tablespoon tomato paste
1 tablespoon sugar
1 tablespoon chopped parsley

Combine onion and celery in shallow dish, cook on HIGH 3 minutes, add tomatoes, cook on HIGH 2 minutes. Blend cornflour and vinegar in bowl, stir in garlic, sauces, water, tomato paste and sugar. Add to tomato mixture, cook on HIGH 5 minutes, stirring once. Add chicken mix well, cook on HIGH 10 minutes. Sprinkle with parsley.
Serves 4.

COLD CHICKEN IN PIMIENTO SAUCE

Canned pimientos are imported and can be bought from delicatessens or gourmet sections of supermarkets.

8 chicken drumsticks
1 tablespoon lemon juice
1 clove garlic, crushed
½ teaspoon dried oregano leaves
PIMIENTO SAUCE
200gm can Sweet Red Pimientos, drained
2 teaspoons tomato paste
½ teaspoon sugar
1 cup mayonnaise
1 tablespoon lemon juice
½ cup thickened cream
1 tablespoon chopped parsley

Combine chicken, lemon juice, garlic and oregano, marinate several hours or refrigerate overnight. Place chicken in single layer in shallow dish, cover, cook on HIGH 10 minutes. Remove chicken; cool. Serve cold with Pimiento Sauce.
Pimiento Sauce: Cut half the pimientos into thin strips, reserve for garnishing. Puree remaining pimientos, tomato paste, sugar, mayonnaise and lemon juice in blender or processor until smooth. Fold in lightly whipped cream and parsley. Garnish chicken with remaining pimiento strips.
Serves 4.

CREAM OF MUSHROOM AND CHICKEN CASSEROLE

Size 15 chicken
2 onions, sliced
125g mushrooms, sliced
15g butter
440g can cream of mushroom soup
⅓ cup mayonnaise
2 teaspoons french mustard
¾ cup sour cream
3 zucchini, sliced
2 tablespoons grated parmesan cheese
2 tablespoons chopped parsley

Cut chicken into serving-sized pieces, remove skin and fat. Place butter in large dish, add onions and mushrooms, cook on HIGH 3 minutes. Stir in undiluted soup, mayonnaise, mustard and cream; add chicken pieces. Cover, cook on HIGH 20 minutes, stirring occasionally. Stir in zucchini, sprinkle with cheese and parsley, cook on HIGH 5 minutes. Cover dish, stand 15 minutes before serving.

Serves 4.

HEARTY FAMILY CHICKEN CASSEROLE

8 chicken thigh fillets
2 large carrots, thinly sliced
2 bay leaves
1 cup chicken stock
¼ cup plain flour
2 tablespoons water
1 cup frozen peas
125g mushrooms, sliced.

Cut fillets in half, place in dish, add carrots, bay leaves and stock, cover, cook on HIGH 10 minutes. Blend flour with water, add to chicken with peas and mushrooms. Cook on HIGH 10 minutes or until chicken is tender; remove bay leaves before serving.

Serves 4 to 6.

CHICKEN POTATO SLICE

1 barbecued chicken
750g potatoes, thickly sliced
15g butter
6 green shallots, chopped
30g butter, extra
1 clove garlic, crushed
2 tablespoons plain flour
⅓ cup water
1 chicken stock cube
⅓ cup dry white wine
½ cup cream
2 teaspoons french mustard
1 tablespoon mayonnaise
½ cup grated tasty cheese
paprika
2 tablespoons chopped parsley

Remove chicken meat from bones, break into bite-sized pieces. Place potatoes in shallow dish, dot with butter, cover, cook on HIGH 9 minutes, or until tender, top with chicken and shallots. Melt extra butter with garlic in bowl on HIGH 30 seconds, stir in flour, water, crumbled stock cube, wine and cream, cook on HIGH 3 minutes, stir in mustard and mayonnaise, pour over chicken, sprinkle with cheese and paprika. Cook on HIGH 5 minutes or until heated through. Sprinkle with parsley before serving.

Serves 6.

CREAMY CHICKEN CURRY

Benedictine adds an unusual flavor to this recipe, brandy is quite a good substitute. Adjust the amount of curry powder according to type used and personal tastes. We served this light curry with mango chutney, sliced banana dipped in lemon juice and coconut and chopped tomatoes and cucumbers tossed in yoghurt with chopped parsley and mint; also some pappadams and boiled rice.

4 chicken breast fillets
30g butter
1 onion, finely sliced
2 teaspoons curry powder
1 teaspoon turmeric
2 tablespoons Benedictine
1 cup chicken stock
2 tablespoons plain flour
2 tablespoons water
¼ cup cream

Cut chicken into thin strips. Combine butter, onion, curry powder and turmeric in dish, cook on HIGH 5 minutes. Stir in chicken, Benedictine and stock, cook on HIGH 8 minutes or until chicken is tender. Remove chicken to serving plate, blend flour with cold water, stir into liquid in dish with cream, cook on HIGH 3 minutes or until sauce boils and thickens. Pour over chicken.

Serves 4.

ABOVE: Creamy Chicken Curry.
OPPOSITE PAGE: Left: Chicken Potato Slice; Right: Hearty Family Chicken Casserole; Back: Cream of Mushroom and Chicken Casserole.

BEEF AND LAMB

Choose good quality, lean, tender cuts of beef and lamb for cooking in the microwave oven. Trim away as much fat and sinew as possible before cooking. Cover loosely with plastic food wrap and stand for times indicated in individual recipes.

LAMB CUTLETS WITH BLUE CHEESE TOPPING
8 lamb cutlets
2 teaspoons french mustard
2 cloves garlic, peeled
90g blue vein cheese
15g butter
1 teaspoon lemon juice
1 tablespoon chopped parsley

Trim fat from cutlets, spread one side of each cutlet with mustard. Insert a sliver of garlic between bone and meat in each cutlet. Place cutlets in shallow dish so the bones are towards the centre of the dish. Cook on HIGH 3 minutes. Spread each cutlet with combined cheese, butter, lemon juice and parsley. Cook on HIGH 2 minutes.

Serves 4.

HONEYED RACKS OF LAMB
4 racks lamb (3 cutlets each)
1 clove garlic, peeled
1 tablespoon soy sauce
1 tablespoon dry sherry
1 tablespoon honey

Trim fat from lamb, cut deep slits between each cutlet. Cut garlic into thin slivers, place a sliver between each cutlet. Combine soy sauce, sherry and honey, brush over lamb, place on plate or turntable, cook on HIGH 10 to 15 minutes, or until done as desired. Baste several times during cooking.

Serves 4.

FRESH HERBED LAMB CASSEROLE

Medium High cooking allows time for the fresh herb flavors to develop. Dried herbs can be used if necessary in the proportion of 1 teaspoon dried to 2 tablepoons fresh. Ask the butcher to remove the bone from the leg of lamb.

1 small leg of lamb, boned (about 1kg)
2 bacon rashers, chopped
1 onion, quartered
1 clove garlic, crushed
2 medium potatoes, chopped
2 medium carrots, sliced
1 tablespoon chopped thyme
2 tablespoons chopped mint
2 tablespoons chopped basil
½ cup chicken stock
1 tablespoon plain flour
1 tablespoon tomato paste
1 cup frozen (or fresh) peas

Remove fat from lamb, cut lamb into 2.5cm pieces. Combine bacon, onion and garlic in bowl, cook on HIGH 5 minutes, or until onion is tender; add lamb, potatoes, carrots and herbs. Blend flour with stock, stir in tomato paste, stir into meat mixture. Cook, covered, on MEDIUM HIGH 20 minutes, stirring occasionally. Stir in peas, cook on HIGH 5 minutes.

Serves 6.

DEVILLED LAMB CHOPS
4 lamb chump chops
2 tablespoons fruit chutney
1 teaspoon curry powder
1 tablespoon brown sugar
2 teaspoons soy sauce
1 teaspoon vinegar

Remove fat from chops, place chops in single layer in shallow dish, top with combined chutney, curry powder, sugar, soy sauce and vinegar. Cook on HIGH 5 minutes or until chops are tender.

Serves 4.

In descending order: Lamb Cutlets with Blue Cheese Topping; Fresh Herbed Lamb Casserole; Curried Lamb; Honeyed Racks of Lamb; Devilled Lamb Chops.

CURRIED LAMB

If a hotter curry is preferred, increase the chilli powder.

1kg lamb leg chops
¼ cup brown vinegar
1 tablespoon soy sauce
¼ teaspoon saffron powder
1 small onion, chopped
½ teaspoon chilli powder
1 tablespoon oil
1 onion, chopped, extra
1 clove garlic, crushed
2 teaspoons grated green ginger
2 tablespoons tomato paste
¾ cup beef stock
1 tablespoon plain flour
2 tablespoons water
2 green shallots, chopped
CURRY POWDER
2 tablespoons coriander seeds
1 tablespoon uncooked rice
2 tablespoons cumin seeds
2 teaspoons mustard seeds
4 cardamom pods
4 whole cloves
2.5cm piece cinnamon stick

Curry Powder: Place all ingredients in blender, blend until finely powdered, about 1 minute. Mixture will make about ½ cup Curry Powder, use 1 tablespoon for this recipe, store remaining Curry Powder in screw-top jar for future use.

Trim fat from meat, remove meat from bones, cut meat into bite-sized pieces. Combine the 1 tablespoon Curry Powder, vinegar, soy sauce, saffron, onion and chilli powder in bowl, add lamb, mix well, stand 1 hour. Place oil, extra onion, garlic and ginger in dish, cook on HIGH 3 minutes. Add meat and marinade, cook on HIGH 3 minutes, stir. Add tomato paste and beef stock, cook on HIGH 12 minutes, mix flour to a smooth paste with water, stir into curry. Cook on HIGH 3 minutes, or until mixture boils and thickens, sprinkle with shallots.

Serves 4.

At back: Corned Beef with Parsley Sauce; Left: Mini Beef Rolls; Right: Beef in Red Wine.

CORNED BEEF WITH PARSLEY SAUCE

1.5kg piece corned beef
2 cups water
2 tablespoons vinegar
2 tablespoons brown sugar
1 onion, quartered
PARSLEY SAUCE
30g butter
1 small onion, chopped
1 tablespoon plain flour
1¼ cups milk
1 tablespoon chopped parsley

Place corned beef into oven bag with water, vinegar, brown sugar and onion, secure loosely with a rubber band. Place into a dish, cook on HIGH 10 minutes, reduce setting to MEDIUM, cook further 30 minutes, turn meat once during cooking. Stand 10 minutes in bag before serving with Parsley Sauce. If serving cold, allow to cool in oven bag.

Parsley Sauce: Combine butter and onion in small bowl, cook on HIGH 2 minutes, or until onion is tender. Add flour, cook on HIGH 30 seconds, stir in milk and parsley, cook on HIGH 3 minutes or until sauce boils.

Serves 4 to 6.

MINI BEEF ROLLS
375g eye fillet steak (in one piece)
¼ cup cornflour
paprika
125g packet cream cheese
2 teaspoons grainy mustard
2 teaspoons horseradish cream
6 gherkins
2 teaspoons worcestershire sauce

Trim fat from steak, cut steak into thin slices. Sprinkle both sides with combined cornflour and paprika. Pound steaks lightly with mallet. Combine cream cheese with mustard and horseradish, spread a teaspoon of mixture onto one side of each steak, top with strips of gherkin. Roll up like a swiss roll. Place rolls seam side down in single layer in shallow dish. Brush with worcestershire sauce. Cook on HIGH 3 minutes or until steak is tender, baste with pan juices during and after cooking.
Serves 4.

LAMB AND VEGETABLES IN AN OVEN BAG

Cooking time given below will give you slightly pink lamb, extend time to 30 minutes if you prefer lamb better done.

1.5kg leg of lamb
10 small carrots
6 baby new potatoes
6 small onions
¼ cup plain flour
2 teaspoons brown sugar
1 teaspoon french mustard
1 clove garlic, crushed
2 teaspoons worcestershire sauce
¼ cup barbecue sauce
¾ cup water

Ask butcher to bone lamb and to trim away excess fat. Trim lamb so that it sits flat. Place lamb and vegetables into large (turkey-sized) oven bag. Cut 2.5cm strip from open end of oven bag. Blend flour, sugar, mustard, garlic, worcestershire sauce and barbecue sauce with water, pour over lamb and vegetable mixture. Tie bag securely with strip. Cut two small holes in bag near tie. Cook on HIGH 25 minutes. Stand 20 minutes before carving lamb (meat will finish cooking during standing time).
Serves 6.

BEEF IN RED WINE
500g rump steak, chopped
2 bacon rashers, chopped
1 large onion, chopped
1 clove garlic, crushed
1 tablespoon plain flour
1 tablespoon tomato paste
1 cup red wine
1 beef stock cube
60g small mushrooms, halved
2 tablespoons chopped parsley

Combine bacon, onion and garlic in shallow dish, cook on HIGH 5 minutes. Stir in flour, steak, tomato paste, wine, crumbled stock cube and mushrooms. Cover, cook on HIGH 15 minutes or until steak is tender. Serve sprinkled with parsley.
Serves 4.

CHINESE LAMB WITH TOMATOES

8 lamb chump chops
1 green pepper
¼ cup water
¼ cup light soy sauce
¼ teaspoon sesame oil
¼ cup dry sherry
1 teaspoon sugar
2 cloves garlic, crushed
2 medium tomatoes
2 tablespoons cornflour
¼ cup water, extra

Cut lamb and pepper into thin strips, combine with water, soy sauce, sesame oil, sherry, sugar and garlic in shallow dish. Cook on HIGH 10 minutes or until meat is tender. Cut tomatoes into wedges, blend cornflour with extra water, add to meat. Cook on HIGH 3 minutes or until sauce boils and thickens and tomatoes are just tender.

Serves 4.

In descending order: Lamb and Vegetables in an Oven Bag; Marinated Racks of Lamb; Chinese Lamb with Tomatoes.

MARINATED RACKS OF LAMB

4 racks of lamb (3 cutlets each)
1 small onion, grated
1 clove garlic, crushed
2 teaspoons worcestershire sauce
2 teaspoons vinegar
2 tablespoons sugar
3 tablespoons chopped mint
½ cup dry white wine
1 teaspoon soy sauce
2 teaspoons cornflour
2 tablespoons water

Remove skin and excess fat from lamb, pierce each rack several times with a fork. Combine onion, garlic, worcestershire sauce, vinegar, sugar, mint and wine in large shallow dish, add lamb, mix well, stand 1 hour, turning occasionally. Remove lamb from marinade. Add blended soy sauce, cornflour and water to marinade, mix well. Cook on HIGH 2 minutes, or until mixture boils and thickens, stir once during cooking. Return lamb to marinade, cook on HIGH 7 minutes or until tender, baste once during cooking. Strain sauce before serving over lamb.

Serves 4.

CREAMY BEEF STROGANOFF

You will find it easy to slice the steak finely if it is partly frozen.

500g rump steak
1 onion, thinly sliced
1 clove garlic, crushed
60g butter
250g mushrooms, sliced
¼ cup plain flour
1 cup beef stock
1 tablespoon dry sherry
1 tablespoon tomato sauce
½ teaspoon worcestershire sauce
½ cup sour cream

Cut steak into fine strips. Combine onion, garlic and butter in dish, cook on HIGH 3 minutes or until onion is tender. Add mushrooms, cook on HIGH 2 minutes. Toss steak in flour, add to dish with stock, sherry and sauces. Cook on HIGH 5 minutes, reduce to MEDIUM HIGH, cook 15 minutes or until meat is tender, stirring occasionally. Stir in sour cream, serve with rice or noodles.

Serves 4.

BRANDIED BEEF WITH MUSHROOMS

500g scotch fillet (in one piece)
1 teaspoon paprika
30g butter
250g mushrooms, sliced
1 tablespoon brandy
6 green shallots, chopped
1 teaspoon lemon juice
⅓ cup thickened cream
⅓ cup sour cream

Trim fat from steak, cut steak into thin slices, sprinkle with paprika; pound lightly with a mallet. Melt butter in shallow dish on HIGH 30 seconds, add steak, cook on HIGH 1½ minutes. Remove steak from dish. Add mushrooms to juices in dish, cook on HIGH 2 minutes. Add brandy, shallots, lemon juice, cream and sour cream, cook on HIGH 2 minutes or until heated through. Pour over steak.

Serves 4.

In descending order: Brandied Beef with Mushrooms; Creamy Beef Stroganoff; Beef with Black Bean Sauce.

PORK, VEAL, HAM AND BACON

The tender cuts of pork and veal are ideal for cooking in the microwave oven. If using steaks, choose steaks of similar size to ensure even cooking. Don't over-cook, season after cooking — particularly when using ham or bacon in a recipe; cover food only when recipe specifies.

GARLIC PORK WITH BLACK BEANS
4 lean forequarter pork chops
1 tablespoon black beans (see note below)
2 cloves garlic, crushed
2 teaspoons soy sauce
3 teaspoons sugar
2 teaspoons cornflour
1 tablespoon dry sherry
1 teaspoon chilli sauce
1 tablespoon oil
1 green pepper, chopped
1 red pepper, chopped
1 onion, chopped

Remove rind from pork, cut pork into bite-sized pieces. Combine lightly crushed black beans, garlic, soy sauce, sugar, cornflour, sherry and chilli sauce in shallow dish, mix in pork. Drizzle oil over pork. Cook on HIGH 8 minutes, stir after 5 minutes. Add peppers and onion to pork, mix well. Cook on HIGH 3 minutes.
Serves 4.
Note: Chinese black beans can be bought in packets or cans from food stores or Chinese supermarkets.

Back: Garlic Pork with Black Beans; Front: Individual Pork Pizzas; Right: Spareribs in Tangy Tomato Sauce.

SPARERIBS IN TANGY TOMATO SAUCE

1kg pork rashers or spareribs
1 tablespoon oil
1 cup tomato sauce
2 tablespoons water
2 tablespoons brown sugar
1 tablespoon worcestershire sauce
1 clove garlic, crushed
3 tablespoons vinegar
1 tablespoon lemon juice
1 teaspoon paprika
½ teaspoon ground ginger
2 teaspoons soy sauce

Trim spareribs of rind and excess fat, place ribs in a shallow dish. Cook on HIGH 14 minutes, turning halfway through cooking time. Drain fat from dish carefully. Pour combined remaining ingredients over ribs; cook on HIGH 3 minutes or until hot.

Serves 4.

INDIVIDUAL PORK PIZZAS

We used black olives and cherry tomatoes as a topping, try fresh pineapple with stuffed olives or whatever topping ingredients you prefer. Use lean mince, or mince pork fillet.

500g minced pork
¾ cup stale wholemeal breadcrumbs
1 onion, finely chopped
1 clove garlic, crushed
1 teaspoon paprika
¼ teaspoon dried oregano leaves
2 teaspoons soy sauce
½ cup tomato paste
1 teaspoon sugar
½ teaspoon dried basil leaves
90g mushrooms, sliced
1 small green pepper, chopped
12 black olives, sliced
12 cherry tomatoes, sliced
3 slices mozzarella cheese
2 tablespoons grated parmesan cheese

Combine mince, breadcrumbs, onion, garlic, paprika, oregano and soy sauce. Press mixture evenly over base of 6 china saucers (base measures 17cm). Spread evenly with combined tomato paste, sugar and basil, then sprinkle with mushrooms, pepper, olives and tomatoes, top with strips of mozzarella cheese. Sprinkle with parmesan cheese, cook 3 at a time on MEDIUM HIGH 6 minutes, or until mince is cooked. Rotate plates halfway through cooking time, drain away juices, serve immediately.

Makes 6.

VEAL AND CHEESE SANDWICHES

4 veal steaks
1 onion, sliced
1 clove garlic, crushed
15g butter
2 teaspoons paprika
2 tablespoons cornflour
1 cup (125g) grated swiss cheese
½ cup stale wholemeal breadcrumbs
2 tablespoons chopped fresh basil
4 carrots, sliced
½ cup canned beef consomme
2 tablespoons dry white wine

Combine onion, garlic and butter in shallow dish, cook on HIGH 5 minutes. Toss veal in combined paprika and cornflour, pound thinly with mallet. Cut each steak in two, place half the veal in single layer over onion mixture. Sprinkle with combined cheese, breadcrumbs and basil, top with remaining steaks. Place carrots around veal, add combined undiluted consomme and wine, cover, cook on MEDIUM HIGH 7 minutes, or until carrots and veal are tender.

Serves 4.

VEAL TURNOVERS WITH TOMATO SAUCE

4 veal steaks
4 bacon rashers
2 green shallots
1 carrot
1 zucchini
TOMATO SAUCE
3 tomatoes, peeled, chopped
2 tablespoons tomato paste
¼ cup dry white wine
½ teaspoon dried oregano leaves
1 clove garlic, crushed

Pound veal lightly. Cut bacon in half, place a piece on top of each veal steak. Cut shallots, carrot and zucchini into thin strips, toss together. Place vegetable strips over one half of each steak, fold other side over. Tie veal turnovers loosely with string. Place veal in shallow dish in single layer, cook on MEDIUM 10 minutes, turn once during cooking. Remove string, pour excess juices into Tomato Sauce. Serve over veal.
Tomato Sauce: Combine all ingredients, cook on HIGH 5 minutes or until heated through.

Serves 4.

VEAL ROLLS IN APPLE SAUCE

4 veal steaks
30g butter
¾ cup stale breadcrumbs
½ cup chopped prunes
2 green shallots, chopped
2 apples, peeled, thinly sliced
1 small red pepper, thinly sliced
½ cup dry red wine
2 teaspoons cornflour
1 tablespoon water

Melt butter in bowl on HIGH 30 seconds, add breadcrumbs, prunes and shallots. Pound steaks until slightly flattened, press breadcrumbs onto end of steaks, roll up tightly, place into shallow dish in single layer. Add apples, pepper and wine to dish, cover, cook on HIGH 15 minutes or until veal is tender. Place rolls onto serving plate. Blend cornflour with water, add to apple sauce, cook on HIGH 3 minutes or until sauce boils and thickens, pour over veal rolls.

Serves 4.

MOZZARELLA VEAL FLORENTINE

4 veal steaks
4 spinach leaves, chopped
⅓ cup sour cream
1 tablespoon plain flour
1 clove garlic, crushed
1 tablespoon lemon juice
30g butter
1 tomato, sliced
4 slices mozzarella cheese

Pound steaks lightly. Combine spinach and sour cream in bowl, cook on HIGH 5 minutes or until spinach is just soft; stir in flour. Place veal in shallow dish in single layer, add garlic and lemon juice, dot with butter. Cook on HIGH 4 minutes or until veal is just tender, turn once during cooking. Top veal with spinach mixture, tomato and cheese, cook on HIGH 4 minutes or until cheese has melted.

Serves 4.

In descending order: Veal Turnovers with Tomato Sauce; Veal and Cheese Sandwiches; Veal Rolls in Apple Sauce; Mozzarella Veal Florentine.

HAM STEAKS WITH MUSTARD BUTTER

4 ham steaks
4 rashers bacon
4 canned pineapple slices
4 glace cherries
MUSTARD BUTTER
60g butter
2 teaspoons french mustard
2 teaspoons lemon juice
1 tablespoon chopped parsley
1 tablespoon chopped chives

Remove rind from bacon, roll each rasher, secure with toothpick. Place bacon on plate, cover with absorbent paper, cook on HIGH 2 minutes. Place ham steaks in single layer on plate, top with pineapple, cover with absorbent paper, cook on HIGH 3 minutes, garnish with bacon and cherries; serve with Mustard Butter.

Mustard Butter: Combine softened butter, mustard, lemon juice, parsley and chives.

Serves 4.

CHEESY HAM AND POTATOES

440g can leg ham
440g can baby potatoes, drained
30g butter
1 onion, finely sliced
1 tablespoon plain flour
1½ cups milk
1½ cups (185g) grated tasty cheese
1 tablespoon chopped parsley

CHICKEN AND BACON LETTUCE ROLLS

Cook about ½ cup rice in conventional way for this recipe.

1 chicken breast fillet, finely chopped
4 bacon rashers, chopped
8 large lettuce leaves
5 green shallots, chopped
2 sticks celery, chopped
2 teaspoons french mustard
¼ cup chopped parsley
1½ cups cooked rice
¾ cup (90g) grated swiss cheese

Place bacon between sheets of absorbent paper on plate, cook on HIGH 5 minutes (reserve 1 tablespoon). Place lettuce leaves in shallow dish, cover, cook on HIGH 5 minutes or until just wilted, spread out on absorbent paper to drain. Combine chicken, shallots, (reserve 2 tablespoons) and celery in bowl, cook on HIGH 5 minutes, add to chicken mixture with bacon, mustard, parsley and rice, mix well. Place spoonfuls of mixture on lettuce leaves, roll up, place in shallow dish. Sprinkle with cheese and reserved bacon and shallots. Cook on HIGH 5 minutes or until heated through.

Serves 4.

Back, left: Ham Steaks with Mustard Butter; Back, right: Cheesy Ham and Potatoes; Front: Chicken and Bacon Lettuce Rolls.

Mini Terrines with Red Currant Glaze

MINI TERRINES WITH RED CURRANT GLAZE

Terrines can be cooked several days in advance and served cold, or served immediately after cooking.

6 bacon rashers
250g ham
250g lean minced pork
¾ cup stale wholemeal breadcrumbs
1 egg
½ cup cream
1 teaspoon grainy mustard
1 tablespoon horseradish cream
2 tablespoons chopped parsley
90g pistachio nuts, shelled, chopped
RED CURRANT GLAZE
½ cup red currant jelly
2 tablespoons port
2 tablespoons orange juice
1 teaspoon french mustard

Line 6 individual dishes (½ cup capacity) with bacon. Mince ham, combine with pork, breadcrumbs, egg, cream, mustard, horseradish, parsley and pistachios. Pack mixture into dishes. Cook on MEDIUM HIGH 5 minutes, or until meat is cooked through. Stand 10 minutes before turning out. Serve topped with Red Currant Glaze.

Red Currant Glaze: Combine all ingredients in bowl, cook on HIGH 4 minutes, strain, stand 10 minutes, or until glaze begins to thicken.

Cut ham and potatoes into bite-sized pieces. Combine butter and onion in shallow dish, cook on HIGH 4 minutes, or until onion is tender. Add flour, cook on HIGH 1 minute, blend in milk, cook on HIGH 4 minutes or until mixture boils and thickens, stirring occasionally. Add potatoes, ham, cheese and parsley, cook on HIGH 3 minutes or until heated.

Serves 4.

PORK FILLET IN CREAMY PRUNE SAUCE

500g pork fillet
½ cup chopped prunes
½ cup dry white wine
2 tablespoons plain flour
1 tablespoon red currant jelly
300ml carton cream
1 tablespoon lemon juice
1 cup chicken stock
2 tablespoons chopped parsley

Slice pork thinly. Combine prunes and wine in small, shallow dish, cook on HIGH 5 minutes. Place pork in deep dish, mix with flour, add prune mixture, red currant jelly, cream, lemon juice and stock. Cook on HIGH 10 minutes, or until pork is tender, sprinkle with parsley.

Serves 4.

PORK IN ORANGE SAUCE

500g pork fillet
¼ cup plain flour
½ teaspoon dried rosemary leaves
2 teaspoons dry mustard
30g butter
1 large onion, sliced
1 orange
¼ cup dry white wine
½ cup orange juice
¼ cup cream
1 tablespoon chopped parsley

Cut pork into 1cm-thick slices, toss in combined flour, rosemary and mustard. Combine butter and onion in shallow dish, cook on HIGH 4 minutes. Segment orange. Add pork, wine, orange juice and cream to pan, cover, cook on HIGH 6 minutes or until pork is tender. Stir in orange segments and parsley.

Serves 4.

RIGHT:
Back: Bacon and Mushroom Mornay;
Front: Ham and Leeks with Mornay
Sauce.

BELOW:
Back: Pork Fillet in Creamy Prune Sauce;
Right: Pork in Orange Sauce; Front:
Glazed Honeyed Pork Fillet.

GLAZED HONEYED PORK FILLET

750g (about 4) pork fillets
1 tablespoon tomato sauce
2 tablespoons honey
pinch five-spice powder
2 teaspoons soy sauce
SAUCE
2 teaspoons cornflour
½ cup chicken stock
1 tablespoon dry sherry
1 teaspoon sugar
½ teaspoon oyster sauce

Combine tomato sauce, honey, five-spice powder and soy sauce in shallow dish, mix in pork. Cook on HIGH 10 minutes or until tender, basting several times during cooking. Serve pork sliced, with Sauce.

Sauce: Blend cornflour with stock in bowl, add remaining ingredients, cook on HIGH 2 minutes.

Serves 4.

HAM AND LEEKS WITH MORNAY SAUCE

8 slices shoulder ham
2 leeks, thinly sliced
3 tablespoons water
30g butter
3 green shallots, chopped
2 teaspoons capers, chopped
1 tablespoon lemon juice
⅔ cup grated swiss cheese
2 tablespoons grated parmesan cheese
300ml carton thickened cream

Place leeks in dish with water, cook, covered, on HIGH 10 minutes or until leeks are tender; drain. Divide leeks between ham slices and roll up. Place butter in shallow dish, add shallots, capers and lemon juice, cook, on HIGH 2 minutes. Place ham rolls, seam side down, on top of shallot mixture. Combine cheeses and cream in bowl, cook, on HIGH 2 minutes or until cheese is melted. Pour sauce over ham, cook on HIGH 4 minutes or until heated through.

Serves 4.

BACON AND MUSHROOM MORNAY

2 bacon rashers, finely chopped
1 onion, finely chopped
30g butter
2 tablespoons plain flour
1 cup milk
425g can tuna, drained
¼ cup cream
1 tablespoon chopped parsley
185g mushrooms, finely sliced
½ cup grated tasty cheese

Place bacon, onion and butter in dish, cook on HIGH 4 minutes, stir in flour then milk, cook on HIGH 3 minutes or until sauce boils and thickens, stirring occasionally. Stir in tuna, cream, parsley and mushrooms. Divide mixture between 4 individual dishes, sprinkle with cheese. Cook on HIGH 4 minutes or until cheese is melted.

Serves 4.

This section includes a great variety of vegetable dishes — vegetable accompaniments, vegetarian dishes and some recipes in which the main ingredient is vegetables, pasta or rice, with the addition of a little seafood or meat. These recipes are particularly good to try on the family if you are cutting down on meat consumption. In some recipes it is quicker and easier to boil rice or pasta in the conventional way rather than cook it in the microwave oven. Follow individual recipes for instructions. The color and flavor of vegetables are unbeatable when cooked in the microwave oven. To cook vegetables (frozen or fresh) such as peas, beans, broccoli or carrots, simply place them into a large shallow dish in an even layer; add about two tablespoons water, cover the dish with plastic food wrap or a lid, cook on HIGH for about 5 minutes. Time depends on type and amount of vegetables. Be careful of steam when removing the plastic food wrap. To cook jacket potatoes; wash and dry them, prick skin all over, place around outside edge of turntable, cook on HIGH until just tender. Time depends on size and number of potatoes e.g. one large potato takes about 5 minutes, 4 large, about 12 minutes.

HOT POTATO BEAN SALAD
500g potatoes, thinly sliced
1 large apple, sliced
250ml carton apple juice
440g can red kidney beans, drained
3 green shallots, chopped
Place potato and apple slices into shallow dish, pour over apple juice, cover, cook on HIGH 5 minutes or until potatoes are tender. Stir in beans, heat on HIGH 3 minutes, sprinkle with shallots.
    Serves 4 to 6.

Back: Scalloped Potatoes and Carrots.
Centre from left: Gingered Sweet
Potatoes with Orange: Hot Potato Bean
Salad: Cheese and Chilli Vegetable
Puree. Front from left: Scalloped
Potatoes with Bacon; Stuffed Jacket
Potatoes.

GINGERED SWEET POTATOES WITH ORANGE

Try this with any roast; it's a traditional accompaniment to turkey in North America.

2 sweet potatoes, peeled, sliced
¼ cup orange juice
1 tablespoon honey
15g butter
1 tablespoon brown sugar
2 teaspoons grated fresh ginger
1 orange, thinly sliced
CRUNCHY PECAN TOPPING
¼ cup stale wholemeal breadcrumbs
2 tablespoons brown sugar
¼ teaspoon cinnamon
60g pecan nuts

Place potatoes in single layer over base of greased shallow dish. Top with combined orange juice, honey, butter, sugar, ginger, cover; cook on HIGH 6 minutes, or until potatoes are tender. Place orange slices between potatoes, sprinkle with Topping, cook on HIGH 3 minutes, or until heated.
Crunchy Pecan Topping: Combine all dish. Cook on HIGH 3 minutes, stirring occasionally.
Serves 4 to 6.

SCALLOPED POTATOES AND CARROTS

1kg old potatoes, peeled, sliced
2 carrots, peeled, sliced
2 tablespoons water
60g packaged cream cheese
⅓ cup milk
1 clove garlic, crushed
¼ cup grated parmesan cheese
1 tablespoon chopped chives

Layer potatoes and carrots in dish, add water, cover, cook on HIGH 10 minutes or until vegetables are just tender. Beat cream cheese, milk, garlic and half the cheese together. Pour over potatoes, sprinkle with remaining cheese, cook on HIGH 4 minutes. Sprinkle with chives.
Serves 6.

SCALLOPED POTATOES WITH BACON

500g potatoes, thinly sliced
4 bacon rashers, chopped
3 green shallots, chopped
300g carton sour cream
1 cup grated tasty cheese

Place potato slices evenly into shallow dish, cover, cook on HIGH 10 minutes or until potatoes are tender, drain. Combine bacon and shallots in small dish, cover with absorbent paper, cook on HIGH 2 minutes or until slightly soft. Spread sour cream over potatoes, top with bacon mixture and cheese. Cook on HIGH 5 minutes or until heated through and cheese melted.
Serves 4 to 6.

CHEESE AND CHILLI VEGETABLE PUREE

Adjust chilli sauce to suit your taste; strength depends on type used.

750g potatoes, peeled
750g pumpkin, peeled
1 large onion, chopped
¼ cup water
30g butter
1 teaspoon chilli sauce
2 green shallots, chopped
½ cup grated tasty cheese
1 tablespoon chopped parsley

Cut potatoes and pumpkin into small cubes, place in shallow dish with onion and water. Cover, cook on HIGH 10 minutes or until vegetables are tender. Drain, press through sieve. Add butter, chilli sauce and shallots to sieved mixture, divide between 4 individual dishes, sprinkle with cheese. Reheat on HIGH 3 minutes or until cheese is melted, sprinkle with parsley.
Serves 4.

STUFFED JACKET POTATOES
4 medium potatoes
oil
salt
30g butter
⅓ cup sour cream
4 green shallots, chopped
1 tablespoon chopped parsley
1 tablespoon grated tasty cheese
paprika

Pierce potato skins all over with fork, rub with oil and salt, place around outer edge of turntable, cook on HIGH 10 minutes or until tender, stand 10 minutes. Slice tops from potatoes, scoop pulp from shells. Mash pulp with butter, sour cream, shallots and parsley. Spoon mixture back into shells. Sprinkle with cheese and paprika, cook on HIGH 2 minutes, or until heated through.
Serves 4.

LAYERED POTATO CASSEROLE
500g old potatoes, thinly sliced
2 onions, thinly sliced
3 tomatoes, sliced
3 carrots, thinly sliced
½ cup chicken stock
15g butter
1 tablespoon chopped parsley

Line base of deep dish with a single layer of potato, then a layer of onion, tomato and carrot. Repeat layering until all vegetables are used, finishing with a layer of potatoes. Pour stock into dish, dot with butter, cover, cook on HIGH 15 minutes or until vegetables are tender, sprinkle with parsley before serving.
Serves 4.

Back from left: Layered Potato Casserole; Curried Corn and Bacon with Mixed Vegetables. Front: Chinese Vegetables in Sate Sauce.

58

CURRIED CORN AND BACON WITH MIXED VEGETABLES

2 bacon rashers, chopped
440g can corn kernels, drained
¼ cup cream
½ teaspoon curry powder
500g packet frozen mixed vegetables

Cook bacon between sheets of absorbent paper on HIGH 2 minutes. Place corn in shallow dish, add bacon, cream, curry powder and vegetables. Cook, covered on HIGH 7 minutes.

Serves 6.

CHINESE VEGETABLES IN SATE SAUCE

30g chinese dried mushrooms
1 tablespoon oil
1 teaspoon grated fresh ginger
200g snow peas, topped and tailed
1 red pepper, chopped
425g can baby corn cuts, drained
1½ tablespoons cornflour
1 cup chicken stock
2 teaspoons sate sauce
2 cups (125g) bean sprouts
2 green shallots, chopped

Place mushrooms in small bowl, cover with hot water, cook on HIGH 5 minutes or until mushrooms are soft. Stand 5 minutes, drain, discard stalks, chop caps roughly.

Combine oil, ginger, snow peas and pepper in deep dish, cook on HIGH 4 minutes or until vegetables begin to soften. Add mushrooms, corn, blended cornflour and stock and sate sauce to vegetables. Cook on HIGH 3 minutes or until mixture boils and thickens, stirring occasionally. Stir in bean sprouts and shallots, heat on HIGH 1 minute.

Serves 4.

LEMONY GREEN BEANS

500g fresh green beans
1 cup chicken stock
30g butter
1 onion, finely chopped
1 clove garlic, crushed
1 tablespoon plain flour
1 tablespoon lemon juice

String and cut beans into 2.5cm lengths. Place into shallow dish with stock, cover, cook on HIGH 8 minutes or until beans are tender; drain, reserve stock. Place butter, onion and garlic in dish, cook on HIGH 4 minutes or until onion is tender. Stir in flour, then lemon juice and reserved stock, cook on HIGH 3 minutes or until mixture boils and thickens, stirring once. Combine beans with hot sauce. Reheat 2 minutes on HIGH if necessary.

Serves 4.

SHREDDED ZUCCHINI AND CORN SAUTE

1 small red pepper
30g butter
3 large zucchini, grated
440g can corn kernels, drained
2 teaspoons honey
1 tablespoon chopped parsley

Cut red pepper into thin strips, place in dish, add butter, cook on HIGH 2 minutes, or until pepper is tender. Add zucchini and corn, cook on HIGH 2 minutes or until zucchini is tender, stir in honey and parsley. Serve hot or cold.

Serves 4.

TASTY TOMATO AND PINENUT CASSEROLE

2 bacon rashers, finely chopped
½ cup pinenuts
4 tomatoes, peeled, sliced
1 onion, sliced
2 tablespoons chopped parsley
½ teaspoon dried mixed herbs
½ cup grated tasty cheese

Cook bacon between sheets of absorbent paper on HIGH 5 minutes. Place pinenuts in shallow dish, cook on HIGH 5 minutes or until lightly toasted (reserve 2 tablespoons pinenuts) stir in bacon, parsley and herbs. Alternate layers of tomatoes, onion and pinenut mixture in shallow dish. Sprinkle with combined cheese and reserved pinenuts, cover, cook on HIGH 10 minutes or until heated.

Serves 4.

RIGHT:
Back: Tasty Tomato and Pinenut Casserole. Centre: Lemony Green Beans. Front: Shredded Zucchini and Corn Saute.

BELOW:
From left: Bean-Stuffed Onions; Three Bean Tomato Chilli.

BEAN-STUFFED ONIONS

4 medium onions
300g can Three Bean Mix, drained
1 clove garlic, crushed
⅓ cup grated tasty cheese
1 small stick celery, finely chopped
2 tablespoons mayonnaise
1 tablespoon chopped parsley

Remove outer skin from onions, leave small part of root end intact to hold onions together. Place onions in bowl, cover with boiling water, cook, covered on HIGH 7 minutes or until tender; drain, cool. Cut onions in half from root to stem, scoop out centre. Combine beans, garlic, cheese, celery and mayonnaise, divide between onions. Cook onions on HIGH 2 minutes, sprinkle with parsley before serving.

Serves 4.

THREE BEAN TOMATO CHILLI

Adjust chilli powder to suit your family's taste.

1 clove garlic, crushed
1 onion, finely chopped
1 stick celery, chopped
1 teaspoon oil
400g can tomatoes
1 tablespoon tomato paste
440g can red kidney beans, drained
310g can butter beans, drained
440g can yellow butter beans, drained
½ teaspoon chilli powder
1 green pepper, chopped
¼ cup grated tasty cheese
paprika

Combine garlic, onion, celery and oil in dish, cook on HIGH 3 minutes. Add undrained crushed tomatoes, tomato paste, beans, chilli powder and pepper, cook on HIGH 5 minutes, or until mixture boils. Top with cheese, sprinkle lightly with paprika, cook on HIGH 2 minutes or until cheese is melted.

Serves 6 to 8.

EGGS FLORENTINE WITH MUSHROOM SAUCE

6 spinach leaves, chopped
440g can baby potatoes, drained, sliced
4 eggs
1 cup tasty grated cheese
1 tablespoon chopped parsley
MUSHROOM SAUCE
250g mushrooms, sliced
30g butter
1 tablespoon plain flour
¾ cup milk

Place spinach in bowl, cover, cook on HIGH 3 minutes or until just wilted. Place potatoes in shallow dish, top with spinach and Mushroom Sauce. Make four indentations in Sauce, break an egg into each, cover, cook on HIGH 4 minutes or until eggs are almost set. Top with cheese, cook on HIGH 3 minutes or until cheese is melted. Sprinkle with parsley.

Mushroom Sauce: Combine mushrooms and butter in bowl, cook on HIGH 3 minutes or until mushrooms are soft. Stir in flour, cook 1 minute, blend in milk, cook on HIGH 3 minutes or until Sauce boils and thickens, stirring once.

Serves 4.

TOMATO-TOPPED MACARONI CHEESE

Cook 2 cups macaroni for this recipe.

60g butter
2 onions, finely chopped
2 tablespoons plain flour
1½ cups milk
1 cup grated tasty cheese
6 cups cooked macaroni
2 tomatoes, thinly sliced
½ cup grated tasty cheese, extra
2 tablespoons grated parmesan cheese

Combine butter and onions in shallow dish, cook on HIGH 5 minutes or until onions are tender. Add flour, cook on HIGH 1 minute. Blend in milk, cook on HIGH 3 minutes or until mixture boils and thickens, stirring occasionally. Add cheese and macaroni. Pour into deep dish, top with tomato and combined extra cheese and parmesan cheese, cook on HIGH 6 minutes or until heated through.

Serves 4.

VEGERONI STROGANOFF

Vegeroni is available from health food stores and supermarkets. It is a vegetable-flavored pasta.

250g packet vegeroni
15g butter
1 onion, chopped
500g small mushrooms
⅓ cup dry white wine
2 beef stock cubes
1 teaspoon cornflour
⅓ cup water
2 tablespoons tomato paste
300g carton sour cream
2 tablespoons chopped parsley

Place 2 litres hot water in large bowl, cover, bring to boil on HIGH about 10 minutes. Add vegeroni, cook on HIGH 10 minutes; drain.

Combine butter and onion in large bowl, cook on HIGH 2 minutes, add mushrooms and wine, cook on HIGH 5 minutes. Stir in combined crumbled stock cubes, blended cornflour and water, tomato paste, vegeroni and sour cream, cook on HIGH 5 minutes, sprinkle with parsley.

Serves 4.

SPAGHETTI AND SPINACH PIE

185g spaghetti
2½ cups boiling water
2 eggs
250g packet frozen spinach
2 green shallots, chopped
1 egg, extra
2 tablespoons milk
130g can diced peppers, drained
2 tablespoons grated tasty cheese

Break spaghetti in half, place in large bowl, add water, cover, cook on HIGH 8 minutes; drain. Combine spaghetti and lightly beaten eggs. Press spaghetti over base and side of greased pie plate (base measures 18cm). Cover, cook on HIGH 2 minutes or until set. Thaw spinach, drain well. Combine spinach, shallots, lightly beaten extra egg, milk, peppers and cheese. Spoon mixture over spaghetti, cover, cook on HIGH 5 minutes or until set. Stand 5 minutes before cutting.

Serves 4.

HAM, PUMPKIN AND CHEESE CASSEROLE

500g pumpkin, peeled, chopped
125g ham, chopped
2 eggs
¾ cup milk
250g carton cottage cheese
2 tablespoons grated parmesan cheese
¼ teaspoon nutmeg
½ teaspoon cumin
2 tablespoons grated tasty cheese
1 green shallot, chopped

Place pumpkin in shallow dish, cover, cook on HIGH 10 minutes, drain well, return to dish; add ham. Combine eggs, milk, cottage cheese, parmesan cheese, nutmeg and cumin, mix well, pour over pumpkin. Sprinkle with cheese and shallot; cover, cook on MEDIUM LOW 15 minutes, turning dish several times during cooking.

Serves 4.

CARROTS WITH CURRY CORIANDER SAUCE

500g baby carrots, peeled
½ cup chicken stock
1 onion, finely chopped
30g butter
1 tablespoon plain flour
½ cup milk
2 teaspoons tomato paste
1 teaspoon curry powder
2 tablespoons chopped fresh coriander

Combine carrots and stock in dish, cover, cook on HIGH 7 minutes, or until carrots are tender, drain, reserve stock. Combine onion and butter in bowl, cook on HIGH 3 minutes, stir in flour, then milk, reserved stock, tomato paste and curry powder. Cook on HIGH 3 minutes or until mixture boils and thickens; stir once during cooking. Stir in coriander, pour over carrots, reheat on HIGH 2 minutes.

Serves 4.

*Back: Tomato-Topped Macaroni Cheese.
Centre from left: Eggs Florentine with
Mushroom Sauce; Vegeroni Stroganoff.
Front: Spaghetti and Spinach Pie.*

63

CREAMY BASIL CHOKOS

3 chokos, peeled
3 rashers bacon, finely chopped
1 onion, finely chopped
½ cup thickened cream
2 tablespoons chopped fresh basil
2 tablespoons grated parmesan
   cheese

Cut chokos into eighths. Place bacon and onion in shallow dish, cook on HIGH 5 minutes. Add chokos, cover, cook on HIGH 5 minutes or until chokos are tender. Top with combined cream, basil and cheese, cook on HIGH 2 minutes.

    Serves 4 to 6.

CABBAGE WITH TOMATO AND HAM

¼ savoy cabbage, shredded
2 tablespoons water
400g can tomatoes
1 clove garlic, peeled
3 tablespoons grated parmesan
   cheese
125g ham
1 tablespoon chopped parsley

Place cabbage and water in bowl, cover, cook on HIGH 6 minutes. Combine undrained tomatoes, garlic and cheese in blender, blend 30 seconds; Pour over cabbage. Cut ham into thin strips, stir through cabbage with parsley, cover, cook on HIGH 1 minute.

    Serves 6.

INSTANT VEGETARIAN PIZZA

2 rounds lebanese flat bread
2 tablespoons tomato paste
3 medium tomatoes, peeled, sliced
1 large new potato, grated
1 onion, chopped
1 red pepper, chopped
125g small mushrooms
10 stuffed olives, sliced
250g mozzarella cheese, grated
2 tablespoons grated parmesan
   cheese

Spread bread with tomato paste, top with tomato, then potato; sprinkle with onion, pepper, mushrooms and olives. Sprinkle with combined cheeses, cook one at a time on HIGH 8 minutes or until potato is tender and cheese melted.

Back: Cabbage with Tomato and Ham.
Centre from left: Creamy Basil Chokos;
Ham, Pumpkin and Cheese Casserole;
Instant Vegetarian Pizza. Front: Carrots
with Curry Coriander Sauce.

SPEEDY RATATOUILLE

1 small eggplant, sliced
salt
1 tablespoon oil
1 onion, chopped
1 clove garlic, crushed
2 tomatoes, peeled, chopped
¼ cup tomato paste
1 red pepper, chopped
4 zucchini, chopped
1 tablespoon chopped fresh basil
½ teaspoon dried oregano leaves
¼ cup chopped parsley

Sprinkle eggplant with salt on both sides, stand on wire rack 20 minutes, rinse under cold water, dry on absorbent paper. Combine oil, onion and garlic in large bowl, cook on HIGH 4 minutes, mix in eggplant, tomatoes, tomato paste, zucchini, pepper, basil, oregano and half the parsley. Cook on HIGH 10 minutes or until zucchini is just tender. Stir several times during cooking. Sprinkle with remaining parsley before serving.

Serves 4 to 6.

VEGETARIAN MOUSSAKA

2 eggplants, sliced
salt
500g potatoes, thinly sliced
375g zucchini, thinly sliced
310g can Tomato Supreme
3 green shallots, chopped
60g butter
¼ cup plain flour
1½ cups milk
½ cup grated tasty cheese
1 egg
2 tablespoons grated parmesan
   cheese

Sprinkle both sides of eggplant slices with salt, stand on rack, stand 20 minutes, rinse under cold water, pat dry with absorbent paper. Place potatoes in shallow dish, cover, cook on HIGH 5 minutes, drain. Top with zucchini, eggplant, Tomato Supreme and shallots, cover, cook on HIGH 5 minutes or until vegetables are just tender. Melt butter in small bowl on HIGH 1 minute, stir in flour, cook on HIGH 1 minute. Blend in milk, cook on HIGH 3 minutes or until mixture boils and thickens, stirring once; stir in cheese and egg. Pour sauce over vegetable mixture, sprinkle with parmesan cheese, cook on HIGH 6 minutes until heated through and vegetables tender.

Serves 4 to 6.

FRESH PEAS WITH LETTUCE

1kg fresh peas, shelled
1 small onion, finely chopped
1 teaspoon water
15g butter
¼ lettuce, finely chopped
1 tablespoon chopped mint
¼ cup chicken stock
1 teaspoon cornflour
1 tablespoon cream

Combine onion and water in bowl, cook, covered on HIGH 2 minutes. Add butter and peas, cover, cook on HIGH 10 minutes or until peas are just tender. Stir in lettuce, mint, stock and blended cornflour and cream. Cook, covered on HIGH 4 minutes or until mixture boils.

Serves 6.

RIGHT:

Back: Broccoli, Rice and Creamy Mushroom Casserole. Centre from left: Vegetable Risotto; Curried Vegetable and Rice Medley. Front from left: Quick Cook Wheat with Lemon and Parsley; Fried Rice with Barbecued Pork.

BELOW:

Back from left: Speedy Ratatouille; Vegetarian Moussaka. Front: Fresh Peas with Lettuce.

VEGETABLE RISOTTO
1 onion, chopped
2 sticks celery, chopped
30g butter
1 cup long grain rice
½ cup dry white wine
2 cups chicken stock
1 red pepper, chopped
1 green pepper, chopped
4 green shallots, chopped
1 tablespoon chopped parsley
¼ teaspoon turmeric

Combine onion, celery and butter in large shallow dish, cook on HIGH 3 minutes, add rice, wine and stock, cook on HIGH 15 minutes or until rice is tender. Stir occasionally during cooking. Add peppers, shallots, parsley and turmeric, cook on HIGH 2 minutes or until heated through.

Serves 4 to 6.

BROCCOLI, RICE AND CREAMY MUSHROOM CASSEROLE

Boil about ⅔ cup brown rice for 20 to 30 minutes in conventional way.

440g can cream of mushroom soup
300g carton sour cream
1 teaspoon horseradish cream
2 teaspoons worcestershire sauce
1 teaspoon french mustard
¼ cup chopped parsley
1 small red pepper, chopped
1½ cups (185g) grated tasty cheese
2 cups cooked brown rice
500g broccoli

Combine undiluted soup, sour cream, horseradish cream, worcestershire sauce, mustard, parsley, pepper and 1 cup of the cheese. Cut broccoli into flowerets. Layer rice, broccoli and soup mixture into dish, sprinkle with remaining cheese. Cook on HIGH 8 minutes or until broccoli is tender.

Serves 6.

CURRIED VEGETABLE AND RICE MEDLEY

Cook about ⅔ cup rice in conventional way for this recipe.

1 small red pepper
2 carrots
250g broccoli
2 teaspoons oil
1 onion, chopped
1 clove garlic, crushed
1 teaspoon curry powder
1 teaspoon dried cumin
2 tablespoons fruit chutney
125g small mushrooms, sliced
½ cup water
2 cups cooked rice

Cut pepper and carrots into strips, cut broccoli into flowerets. Combine oil and onion in large shallow dish, cook on HIGH 2 minutes, add garlic, curry powder and cumin, cook on HIGH 1 minute, stir in chutney. Stir in pepper, carrot, mushrooms, broccoli and water, cover, cook on HIGH 5 minutes, or until vegetables are tender. Stir in rice, cook on HIGH 2 minutes or until heated through.

Serves 4.

FRIED RICE WITH BARBECUED PORK

Boil about ½ cup brown or white rice in conventional way for this recipe. Buy barbecued pork from your local chinese food store or restaurant.

2 eggs
½ teaspoon sesame oil
30g butter
1 teaspoon grated fresh ginger
1 clove garlic, crushed
3 green shallots, chopped
1 red pepper, chopped
1½ cups cooked rice
250g chinese barbecued pork, (or ham) chopped
2 spinach leaves, shredded
2 teaspoons soy sauce

Beat eggs with sesame oil, pour into pie plate, cook on HIGH 1 minute, pull cooked edges into centre with a fork, cook on HIGH 1 minute or until set, cool, chop finely. Combine butter, ginger, garlic, shallots and pepper in shallow dish, cook on HIGH 1 minute, add rice, pork, egg, spinach and soy sauce, toss well, cook on HIGH 5 minutes or until heated through.
Serves 4.

BROWN RICE WITH PARSLEY AND LEMON

Boil about ¾ cup brown rice in conventional way for this recipe.

1 onion, finely chopped
1 clove garlic, crushed
1 teaspoon oil
2 cups cooked brown rice
1 cup chopped parsley
1 small green pepper, chopped
½ cup grated tasty cheese
¾ cup thickened cream
1 teaspoon grated lemon rind
2 teaspoons lemon juice

Add onion mixture to large bowl with brown rice, parsley, pepper, cheese, cream, lemon rind and juice; mix well. Cook on HIGH 2 minutes or until heated through.
Serves 4.

cream, lemon rind and juice, cook on HIGH 2 minutes or until hot.
Serves 4.

ASPARAGUS WITH CURRY HOLLANDAISE

2 bunches asparagus
¼ cup water
15g butter
1 tablespoon plain flour
1 teaspoon curry powder
2 tablespoons lemon juice
1 teaspoon french mustard
300ml carton thickened cream
30g butter, extra

Place asparagus in shallow dish with water, cover, cook on HIGH 5 minutes. Leave covered to keep hot while making sauce.

Place butter in bowl, cook on HIGH 30 seconds, stir in flour, curry powder, lemon juice and mustard, then cream, cook on HIGH 5 minutes. Beat well with a wire whisk or wooden spoon until smooth, gradually beat in extra butter, serve immediately with hot asparagus. If necessary, reheat asparagus on HIGH for 1 minute.
Serves 4.

CREAMY THREE CHEESE FONDUE

Serve fondue with an assortment of crudites, such as broccoli flowerets, snow peas, baby carrots, cherry tomatoes, green beans, mushrooms or cubed crusty bread. Just dip for lunch or supper.

2 cups dry white wine
1 clove garlic, crushed
375g gruyere cheese, grated
250g swiss cheese, grated
125g tasty cheddar cheese, grated
¼ cup plain flour
pinch nutmeg

Combine wine and garlic in large bowl, cook on HIGH 6 minutes, stir in cheeses and flour. Cook on HIGH 6 minutes, stirring every 2 minutes. Pour into heated fondue pot, keep hot over burner. Sprinkle with nutmeg before serving.
Serves 4 to 6.

BROCCOLI WITH LEMON SAUCE

500g broccoli
½ cup water
15g butter
2 teaspoons plain flour
¾ cup cream
2 egg yolks
1 tablespoon lemon juice
¼ cup toasted flaked almonds

Cut broccoli into flowerets, place in dish with water, cover, cook on HIGH 10 minutes, or until broccoli is tender; drain. Place butter and flour in small bowl, cook on HIGH 30 seconds, stir, gradually stir in combined cream, egg yolks and lemon juice, cook on HIGH 1½ minutes, stirring after 1 minute. Pour sauce over broccoli. Serve sprinkled with almonds.
Serves 6.

STUFFED PEPPERS WITH SALMON

2 green peppers
1 onion, chopped
1 stick celery, chopped
220g can red salmon, drained
¼ cup mayonnaise
2 tablespoons chopped parsley
1 cup grated tasty cheese

Cut peppers in half lengthways, remove seeds. Place peppers in shallow dish, cook on HIGH 4 minutes. Combine onion and celery in bowl, cook on HIGH 3 minutes, stir in salmon, mayonnaise, parsley and ¼ cup of the cheese. Spoon mixture into peppers, sprinkle with remaining cheese, cook on HIGH 3 minutes or until cheese is melted.
Serves 4.

STUFFED BABY SQUASH WITH HAM

500g baby squash
125g pressed shoulder ham
60g butter
1 clove garlic, crushed
2 tablespoons chopped parsley
1 teaspoon french mustard
1 tablespoon water

Remove centre from each squash with apple corer. Beat softened butter with garlic, parsley and mustard. Spread a layer of butter mixture over each ham slice. Roll ham tightly, cut crossways into four pieces. Place a ham roll into each squash, place squash in single layer in shallow dish, add water, cover, cook on HIGH 5 minutes or until squash are tender.
Serves 6.

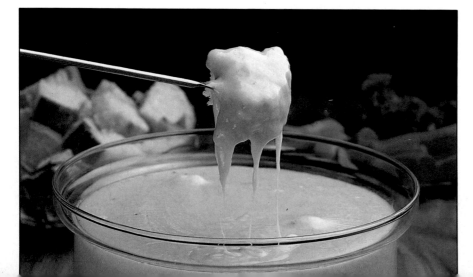

LEFT:
Creamy Three Cheese Fondue

RIGHT:
Back from left: Asparagus with Curry Hollandaise; Broccoli with Lemon Sauce. Front from left: Stuffed Baby Squash with Ham; Stuffed Peppers with Salmon.

DESSERTS

Desserts can be made quickly and easily especially when cooked in individual dishes. These dishes cut down on cooking time and help the desserts to cook more evenly. Always place individual dishes around outside edge of turntable; centralise large single dishes in the oven. Round or oval dishes give better cooking results than square dishes in the microwave oven. We have included two cakes in this section, both of these were cooked in a special microwaveproof ring pan. Remember to turn, cover (loosely with plastic food wrap), stir and stand where indicated in recipes, and remember not to overcook, cooking and setting does continue after the food is removed from the oven.

BRANDIED BANANAS
4 large bananas
60g butter
¾ cup brown sugar, lightly packed
¼ cup cream
2 tablespoons brandy
Place butter and sugar in dish, cook on HIGH 2 minutes. Peel bananas, slice in half lengthwise, add to brown sugar mixture, cook on HIGH 1 minute. Place bananas in serving dishes, stir cream and brandy into sauce, pour over bananas.
   Serves 4.

From left: Apricots with Sour Cream Topping; Caramel Ginger Pears; Brandied Bananas.

CARAMEL GINGER PEARS

4 pears, peeled, quartered
¾ cup dry white wine
¾ cup water
2 teaspoons lemon juice
⅓ cup sugar
1 teaspoon grated fresh ginger
45g butter
½ cup brown sugar, firmly packed

Combine wine, water, lemon juice, sugar and ginger in dish, cook on HIGH 2 minutes. Add pears to wine mixture, cook on HIGH 10 minutes. Drain syrup from pears, reserve ½ cup syrup. Put butter and brown sugar in dish, cook on HIGH 2 minutes, stirring once. Add reserved syrup and pears, reheat on HIGH 1 minute. Serve with cream or icecream.

Serves 4.

APRICOTS WITH SOUR CREAM TOPPING

250g dried apricots
2 cups hot water
⅓ cup sugar
2 passionfruit
300g carton sour cream
1 egg
1 tablespoon sugar, extra
1 passionfruit, extra
cinnamon

Combine apricots and water in bowl, cook on HIGH 15 minutes. Add sugar, stir until dissolved. Puree apricot mixture in blender or processor until smooth, fold in passionfruit pulp. Divide mixture between 4 individual dishes (1 cup capacity). Combine sour cream, egg, extra sugar and pulp from extra passionfruit. Pour over apricot mixture, sprinkle with cinnamon, cook on MEDIUM HIGH 7 minutes. Cool, refrigerate until firm.

Serves 4.

STRAWBERRY RUM CHEESECAKE

125g wheatmeal biscuits, crushed
2 tablespoons ground hazelnuts
1 tablespoon sugar
½ teaspoon cinnamon
90g butter
¼ cup strawberry jam
250g packet cream cheese
2 teaspoons grated lemon rind
1 teaspoon grated orange rind
2 tablespoons rum
2 eggs
⅓ cup sugar, extra
300ml carton thickened cream
250g punnet strawberries

Combine biscuits, hazelnuts, sugar and cinnamon. Place butter in bowl, cook on HIGH 1 minute or until melted, add to biscuit mixture; mix well. Press over base of 20cm flan dish, refrigerate until firm.

Spread with jam. Beat cream cheese on electric mixer until soft, beat in extra sugar, lemon and orange rinds and rum, then eggs, one at a time. Pour mixture over crumb crust. Cook on HIGH 5 minutes, cool, refrigerate until set. Decorate with whipped cream and strawberries.

From left: Strawberry Rum Cheesecake; Pineapple and Lemon Cheesecake.

72

PINEAPPLE AND LEMON CHEESECAKE

60g butter
125g sweet plain biscuits, crushed
250g packet cream cheese
2 eggs
1 teaspoon grated lemon rind
2 tablespoons lemon juice
⅓ cup sugar
450g can crushed pineapple
2 teaspoons gelatine
2 tablespoons water

Place butter in bowl, cook on HIGH 1 minute, or until melted, stir in biscuit crumbs. Press firmly into pie plate (base measures 18cm), cook on HIGH 1 minute, cool.

Beat cream cheese until smooth, beat in eggs, lemon rind, lemon juice and sugar. Drain pineapple, reserve juice, add pineapple to cream cheese mixture, pour into crumb crust. Cook on MEDIUM HIGH 10 minutes, or until just set, cool.

Sprinkle gelatine over water, stir well, cook on HIGH 30 seconds or until gelatine has dissolved. Add to reserved pineapple juice, cool until almost set. Spread over cheesecake, refrigerate until set. Decorate with cream and pineapple if desired.

CREAMED STRAWBERRY RICE

250g punnet strawberries
2 cups white rice
2 cups hot water
2 cups milk
⅓ cup sugar

Mash half the strawberries with a fork, reserve remaining strawberries for decorating.

Wash rice, drain well. Place rice in shallow dish with water and milk. Cook on HIGH 20 minutes or until rice has absorbed all the liquid, stir occasionally during cooking. Stir in sugar and mashed strawberries, reheat on HIGH 2 minutes. Serve hot or cold with cream and reserved strawberries.

Serves 4.

APPLES AND APRICOTS WITH BUTTERSCOTCH CUSTARD

Toast almonds on oven tray in moderate oven 5 minutes.

410g can pie apple
½ cup chopped dried apricots
½ teaspoon cinnamon
2 tablespoons toasted flaked almonds
BUTTERSCOTCH CUSTARD:
½ cup brown sugar
2 tablespoons custard powder
½ cup milk
2 teaspoons butter
1 egg

Combine apple, apricots and cinnamon, divide between four greased individual dishes (½ cup capacity), top with Butterscotch Custard, sprinkle with almonds. Cook on MEDIUM 5 minutes or until custard is just set.

Butterscotch Custard: Combine brown sugar and custard powder in bowl, stir in milk, cook on HIGH 3 minutes, stir once during cooking. Quickly stir in butter and egg, beat until smooth.

Serves 4.

SAUCY MOCHA POTS OF CREAM

2 tablespoons cocoa
1 tablespoon instant coffee powder
1 tablespoon Tia Maria
⅓ cup castor sugar
2 eggs
300ml carton thickened cream

Blend cocoa and coffee with Tia Maria in jug, beat in sugar, eggs and cream. Pour mixture into 6 small individual dishes (⅓ cup capacity), cook on MEDIUM LOW 5 minutes or until just set (mixture should still be very shaky), refrigerate until cold.

Serves 6.

73

APPLE CREAM FLANS

⅓ cup wholemeal plain flour
⅓ cup wholemeal self-raising flour
45g butter
¼ cup brown sugar
1 egg
1 egg yolk, extra
½ cup sour cream
1 teaspoon vanilla
¼ cup brown sugar, extra
2 Granny Smith apples, peeled,
   chopped
cinnamon

Sift flours into basin, rub in butter add sugar. Press mixture over base of 6 individual flan dishes (base measures 9cm). Combine egg, egg yolk, sour cream, vanilla, extra sugar and apples, spoon into flan dishes, sprinkle with cinnamon Cook on MEDIUM HIGH 5 minutes, stand 5 minutes before serving.

PUMPKIN CUSTARD FLANS WITH PECAN TOFFEE

Flans develop better flavor made the day before required and refrigerated overnight. Store leftover Pecan Toffee in an airtight container.

1 cup cooked mashed pumpkin
¾ cup canned sweetened
   condensed milk
1 egg
1 tablespoon cornflour
½ teaspoon mixed spice
2 tablespoons brown sugar
2 tablespoons cold water
PECAN TOFFEE
60g butter
½ cup brown sugar, lightly packed
¼ cup golden syrup
¼ cup chopped pecan nuts

Puree pumpkin, milk, egg, cornflour, spice, sugar and water in blender or processor until smooth. Pour into 6 greased flan dishes (base measure 9 cm). Cook on MEDIUM HIGH 5 minutes. Stand 5 minutes, cover, refrigerate several hours or overnight. Serve with whipped cream and Pecan Toffee.

Pecan Toffee: Combine butter, sugar and syrup in basin, cook on HIGH 6 minutes or until toffee will snap when a teaspoonful of toffee is dropped into a cup of cold water. Add pecans, pour onto greased tray. Chop finely when cold.

LEFT:
Back row from left: Creamed Strawberry Rice; Apples and Apricots with Butterscotch Custard; Middle row from left: Pumpkin Custard Flans with Pecan Toffee; Saucy Mocha Pots of Cream; Front row: Apple Cream Flans.

RIGHT:
In descending order: Peach and Sultana Crunch; Brandy Plum Custard; Rhubarb Strawberry Crumble.

PEACH AND SULTANA CRUNCH

850g can sliced peaches
1½ tablespoons cornflour
2 tablespoons lemon juice
½ cup sultanas
TOPPING
60g butter
½ cup quick cooking oats
¼ cup plain flour
½ cup coconut
½ cup brown sugar, firmly packed
½ teaspoon cinnamon

Drain peaches, reserve syrup. Blend cornflour with lemon juice in pie plate (base measures 18cm), add reserved syrup, cook on HIGH 2 minutes or until mixture boils and thickens. Stir in peaches and sultanas, sprinkle with Topping, cook on HIGH 5 minutes or until bubbly.

Topping: Melt butter in bowl, cook on HIGH 1 minute, stir in remaining ingredients.

   Serves 4 to 6.

BRANDY PLUM CUSTARD

2 x 825g cans plums, drained
teaspoon mixed spice
1 tablespoons brandy
300g carton sour cream
2 eggs

Remove stones from plums, break plums roughly with spoon, place in shallow dish, stir in spice and brandy. Beat cream and eggs together with fork, pour over plums. Cook on HIGH 10 minutes. Stand 5 minutes or until custard is set. Sprinkle with a little extra mixed spice.

   Serves 6.

RHUBARB AND STRAWBERRY CRUMBLE

500g frozen or fresh rhubarb,
   chopped
250g punnet strawberries, halved
1 teaspoon grated orange rind
½ cup brown sugar, firmly packed
2 tablespoons orange juice
2 tablespoons cornflour
TOPPING
½ cup plain flour
½ cup brown sugar, firmly packed
½ cup rolled oats
1 teaspoon cinnamon
60g butter
½ cup chopped pecan nuts.

Place rhubarb in shallow dish, cook on HIGH 4 minutes, drain, add strawberries, orange rind and sugar. Blend orange juice with cornflour, stir into rhubarb mixture, cook on HIGH 7 minutes or until sauce has boiled and thickened, sprinkle with Topping.

Topping: Combine flour, sugar, oats and cinnamon in bowl, rub in butter, mix in pecans. Cook on HIGH 4 minutes, stirring occasionally, stand 5 minutes before sprinkling over rhubarb mixture.

   Serves 4 to 6.

MOIST CARROT CAKE

1 cup self raising wholemeal flour
¾ cup brown sugar, firmly packed
2 teaspoons cinnamon
2 cups finely grated carrot
½ cup chopped raisins
½ cup oil
2 eggs
FROSTING
60g packaged cream cheese
30g butter
1½ cups icing sugar, sifted
2 teaspoons lemon juice
⅓ cup chopped walnuts

Combine flour, sugar, cinnamon, carrot and raisins in bowl, stir in combined oil and eggs. Pour into ungreased base lined 20cm ring cake pan, cook on MEDIUM HIGH 8 minutes, or until just cooked. Stand 5 minutes, turn onto wire rack to cool. Top with Frosting and walnuts.

Frosting: Beat cream cheese and butter until smooth in small bowl of electric mixer, gradually beat in icing sugar and lemon juice.

POPPYSEED HAZELNUT TORTE WITH CHOCOLATE ROUGH GLAZE

⅓ cup poppy seeds
⅓ cup roasted hazelnuts
2 tablespoons self raising flour
4 eggs, separated
⅓ cup brown sugar
300ml carton thickened cream
250g punnet strawberries
CHOCOLATE ROUGH GLAZE
½ cup chopped roasted hazelnuts
125g dark cooking chocolate, chopped
15g butter

Grind poppy seeds, nuts and flour in blender until fine. Beat egg yolks with 2 tablespoons of the sugar on electric mixer until thick and creamy. Beat egg whites until soft peaks form, add remaining sugar, beat until dissolved. Fold poppyseed mixture into egg yolk mixture, fold in egg white mixture. Spoon into lightly greased, base lined 20cm ring pan. Cook on HIGH 3½ minutes, stand 5 minutes before turning out onto wire rack to cool. Reserve ¼ cup of the cream for Chocolate Rough Glaze. Split cake, fill with remaining whipped cream and sliced strawberries, place on serving plate, top with Chocolate Rough Glaze.

Chocolate Rough Glaze: Combine hazelnuts, reserved cream, chocolate and butter in bowl, cook on HIGH 3 minutes, or until chocolate has melted; stir well.

STEAMED DATE PUDDINGS

1 cup finely chopped dates
45g butter
½ cup brown sugar, firmly packed
½ cup water
2 teaspoons vinegar
1 egg
1 tablespoon rum
½ cup plain flour
¼ cup self-raising flour
½ teaspoon bicarbonate of soda
½ teaspoon mixed spice
½ cup milk

Combine dates, butter, brown sugar and water in bowl, cook on HIGH 6 minutes, stirring once during cooking, add vinegar, cool. Stir in combined egg and rum, fold in sifted dry ingredients, alternately with milk. Place mixture into six greased tea cups, cover, cook on MEDIUM-LOW 5 minutes, or until just cooked. Serve hot, with custard, cream or icecream.

Serves 6.

ABOVE:
Back: Poppyseed Hazelnut Torte with Chocolate Rough Glaze; left: Moist Carrot Cake; right: Steamed Date Puddings.

RIGHT:
In descending order: Chocolate Self-Saucing Pudding; Lemon Delicious Puddings; Wholemeal Banana Dumplings in Caramel Sauce.

CHOCOLATE SELF-SAUCING PUDDING

60g butter
1½ cups self raising flour
1 cup castor sugar
¼ cup cocoa
¾ cup milk
2 teaspoons vanilla
1 cup brown sugar, lightly packed
⅓ cup cocoa, extra
2 cups boiling water

Place butter in dish, melt on HIGH for 1 minute, stir in sifted flour, sugar and cocoa, milk and vanilla, beat until smooth with wooden spoon. Sprinkle with combined sifted brown sugar and extra cocoa. Pour boiling water over mixture carefully. Cook on HIGH 12 minutes, or until just cooked in centre; stand 5 minutes before serving with cream or icecream.

Serves 4 to 6.

WHOLEMEAL BANANA DUMPLINGS IN CARAMEL SAUCE

¾ cup self-raising white flour
½ cup self-raising wholemeal flour
30g butter
¼ cup brown sugar
2 very ripe bananas
⅓ cup milk
CARAMEL SAUCE
30g butter
1½ cups brown sugar, firmly packed
1½ cups boiling water

Sift flours into basin, rub in butter, mix in sugar. Peel and mash bananas, mix with milk, add to flour mixture, mix until just combined. Drop tablespoons of dumpling dough into hot Caramel Sauce, cover with lid, cook on HIGH 6 minutes. Stand 5 minutes before serving.

Caramel Sauce: Combine butter, sugar and water in shallow dish. Cook on HIGH 4 minutes or until mixture boils. Stir occasionally during cooking to dissolve sugar.

Serves 4 to 6.

LEMON DELICIOUS PUDDINGS

Toast coconut in pan over heat, stir constantly until golden brown; cool.

45g butter
1 tablespoon grated lemon rind
½ cup castor sugar
4 eggs, separated
⅓ cup plain flour
¾ cup milk
⅓ cup lemon juice
½ cup toasted coconut (see note above)

Cream butter, lemon rind, sugar and egg yolks in small bowl of electric mixer, beat until light and fluffy. Stir in sifted flour, milk and lemon juice. Sprinkle coconut over base and sides of 4 greased individual dishes (1 cup capacity). Beat egg whites until soft peaks form, fold into lemon mixture. Spoon mixture evenly into dishes, sprinkle with remaining coconut, cook on MEDIUM-LOW 4 minutes, serve immediately.

Serves 4.

JAMS AND PICKLES, ETC.

Jams, jellies and butters are great made in a microwave oven. Don't attempt larger quantities than are given here. All fruit — especially citrus rinds — must be tender before adding sugar. Dissolve sugar before the mixture is allowed to boil.

STRAWBERRY JAM

Any berry can be substituted for strawberries, cooking times will vary slightly depending on type used.

2 punnets (500g) strawberries
¼ cup lemon juice
2 cups sugar

Wash and hull strawberries, place in large bowl with lemon juice, cook on HIGH 4 minutes or until soft. Stir in sugar, cook on HIGH 20 minutes or until jam jells when tested on cold saucer; stir occasionally during cooking. Stand 5 minutes before pouring into hot sterilised jars, seal when cold.

Makes about 2 cups.

PROCESSOR LEMON MARMALADE

Any citrus fruit or combination of citrus fruits can be substituted for the lemons. The cooking times will vary depending on type of fruit used.

3 large lemons (500g)
1½ cups water
3 cups sugar

Quarter lemons, discard seeds. Chop lemons finely in processor or blender. Place into deep dish with water, cook on HIGH 10 minutes or until lemon rind is tender. Stir in sugar, cook on HIGH 18 minutes or until jam jells when tested on cold saucer; stir occasionally during cooking. Stand 5 minutes before pouring into hot sterilised jars, seal when cold.

Makes about 2 cups.

CITRUS TOMATO JAM

Do not peel orange and lemon for this recipe.

3 medium (500g) ripe, firm tomatoes
1 small orange, thinly sliced
1 small lemon, thinly sliced
2 cups sugar

Peel and chop tomatoes, discard orange and lemon seeds. Combine tomatoes, orange and lemon in large bowl, cook on HIGH 15 minutes or until rind is tender. Add sugar, stir until dissolved, cook on HIGH 15 minutes, or until mixture jells when tested on a cold saucer, stir several times during cooking. Stand 5 minutes before pouring into hot sterilised jars, seal when cold.

Makes about 2 cups.

Times given are a guide; they vary depending on type of oven and utensil used, and ripeness and water content of fruit. Test often during cooking. Cover jams only when recipe specifies. Store jams, jellies, butters, etc. in cool, dark place, preferably in the refrigerator. Butters keep for up to a month. Jams and jellies, if made correctly, should keep for a year.

We've given a pickle, a chutney and a relish recipe. These are in larger quantities than the jams, etc., so don't attempt at one time any more than recipes state. Cook relishes and chutneys until they are as thick as desired — the cold-saucer test is as good for these as for jam. Store pickles, chutneys and relishes in refrigerator; they keep for up to a month.

APPLE LIME JELLY

Use any type of apples, but sour-tasting apples will give best results, do not peel apples. Use lemon juice if limes are out of season.

6 large (1kg) Granny Smith apples, chopped
3 cups water
3 limes
1½ cups sugar, approximately

From left: Strawberry Jam; Processor Lemon Marmalade; Citrus Tomato Jam; Apple Lime Jelly; Dried Apricot and Passionfruit Conserve.

Squeeze limes, measure ¼ cup juice, combine lime shells with apples and water in large bowl, cover, cook on HIGH 20 minutes. Strain mixture through fine, well wrung-out damp cloth, allow mixture to drip through cloth several hours or overnight; do not squeeze or press mixture through cloth; this gives a cloudy jelly. Measure juice; you should have about 2 cups, return juice to pan. Add ¾ cup sugar to each one cup of juice, stir in lime juice. Cook on HIGH 25 minutes or until mixture jells when tested on a cold saucer. Stir after first 3 minutes to dissolve sugar; then once more after about 10 minutes. Pour mixture into hot sterilised jars, seal when cold.

Makes about 2 cups.

DRIED APRICOT AND PASSIONFRUIT CONSERVE

500g dried apricots
¼ cup lemon juice
2 cups water
4 cups sugar
½ cup passionfruit pulp

Place apricots in large bowl with lemon juice and water, cook on HIGH 15 minutes or until apricots are tender. Add sugar, stir until dissolved, cook on HIGH 10 minutes or until conserve jells when tested on a cold saucer. Stir occasionally during cooking. Add passionfruit, cover, stand 20 minutes stirring occasionally to distribute passionfruit through conserve. Pour into hot sterilised jars, seal when cold.

Makes about 3 cups.

RHUBARB BERRY JAM
Use any fresh or frozen berry of your choice for this jam, we used blackberries.

4 cups (500g) chopped rhubarb, fresh or frozen
3 cups (500g) berries, fresh or frozen
1 teaspoon grated orange rind
1 tablespoon orange juice
1 tablespoon lemon juice
1¾ cups sugar

Combine rhubarb, berries, orange rind, orange juice and lemon juice in large bowl, cover, cook on HIGH 10 minutes. Add sugar, stir until dissolved, cook on HIGH, stirring every 5 minutes, for about 25 minutes, or until jam will jell when tested on a cold saucer. Stand 5 minutes, pour into hot sterilised jars, seal when cold.

Makes about 3 cups.

CITRUS BUTTER
4 eggs
¾ cup sugar
1 teaspoon grated lemon rind
¼ cup lemon juice
1 teaspoon grated orange rind
¼ cup orange juice
¼ cup water
125g butter, chopped

Combine eggs and sugar in bowl, beat with fork, stir in remaining ingredients, cook on HIGH 3 minutes, stir, then cook further 6 minutes on MEDIUM until mixture thickens. Pour into hot sterilised jars, seal when cold.

Makes about 2 cups.

LEFT: Above: Rhubarb Berry Jam.
Below: Citrus Butter.

OPPOSITE PAGE: From left: Corn Chilli Relish; Mixed Pickled Vegetables, Green Tomato Chutney.

CORN CHILLI RELISH

¾ cup sugar
¼ cup brown sugar
2 tablespoons cornflour
2 tablespoons salt
1 tablespoon dry mustard
1 teaspoon turmeric
1½ cups white vinegar
1 cup shredded cabbage
1 small green pepper, chopped
1 small red pepper, chopped
2 medium onions, chopped
1 small red chilli, finely chopped
2 cups (250g) frozen or fresh corn
  kernels

Blend dry ingredients in large bowl with vinegar, add vegetables. Cook on HIGH, 20 minutes, stirring occasionally. Pour mixture into hot sterilised jars, seal when cold.

  Makes about 4 cups.

MIXED PICKLED VEGETABLES

4 sticks celery
2 large carrots
4 large zucchini
1 large onion
1½ cups white vinegar
1 cup sugar
1 teaspoon dry mustard
1 tablespoon whole black
  peppercorns
¼ teaspoon turmeric

Cut celery, carrots and zucchini into thin strips, cut onion into eighths. Combine remaining ingredients in large shallow dish, cook on HIGH 4 minutes. Add vegetables, cook on HIGH 4 minutes or until mixture boils. Strain liquid and reserve. Pack vegetables into hot sterilised jars, pour liquid over, seal when cold.

  Makes about 3 cups.

GREEN TOMATO CHUTNEY

1kg green tomatoes, chopped
2 large onions, chopped
2 large Granny Smith apples,
  peeled, chopped
½ cup cornflour
1½ cups sugar
1½ cups water
1 cup brown vinegar
2 teaspoons turmeric
½ teaspoon cayenne pepper

Blend cornflour and sugar with water in large shallow dish, add remaining ingredients, cover, cook on HIGH 10 minutes. Remove cover, cook on HIGH 20 minutes or until chutney reaches desired consistency; stir occasionally. Pour into hot sterilised jars, seal when cold.

  Makes about 8 cups.

SWEET THINGS

Sweets making is easy in the Microwave oven, providing directions are followed carefully. Make only the quantities given in the recipe at one time; always use a deep bowl. It is important the sugar be dissolved by stirring before the mixture boils. Once the sugar is dissolved, do not stir anymore, but tilt the basin several times during the cooking (see picture below).

Melting chocolate also needs care; it often appears to be solid after a minute or two, but a quick stir is all that is needed. Slices sometimes benefit from being cooked on an upturned saucer, this simply directs the microwaves to the centre underneath (particularly in a square dish) for more even cooking.

Liquid glucose is available in supermarkets, health food stores and chemists. There is no substitute for it in the following recipes.

Choose an ovenproof dish when following sweets recipes, the syrups reach high temperatures.

ALMOND BRITTLE
1 cup sugar
½ cup liquid glucose
¾ cup (100g) slivered almonds
30g butter
1 teaspoon vanilla
1 teaspoon bicarbonate of soda

Combine sugar, glucose and almonds in deep 2 litre dish. Cook on HIGH 11 minutes or until golden brown, stirring occasionally. To test if toffee is cooked, drop a teaspoon of syrup into a cup of cold water. It will set immediately, then crack when snapped between fingers. Stir in butter, vanilla and soda, spread into a shallow 23cm square tin; allow to set. Break into bite-sized pieces, store in an airtight container.

CREAMY CARAMELS
1½ cups brown sugar, firmly packed
¼ cup liquid glucose
300ml carton cream
60g butter
2 teaspoons vanilla

Combine all ingredients in deep 3 to 4 litre dish, cook on HIGH 5 minutes, stirring occasionally to dissolve sugar. Continue cooking, without stirring, for 18 minutes on HIGH or until caramel is dark golden brown. To test if caramel is cooked, drop a teaspoon of syrup into a cup of cold water. It will set immediately, then crack when snapped between fingers. Pour into greased 20cm square cake tin. When partly set, mark into squares. Cut when cold, store in an airtight container.

CREAM CHEESE FUDGE
125g packet cream cheese
1 tablespoon milk
1 teaspoon vanilla
2½ cups icing sugar
200g dark cooking chocolate, chopped
½ cup chopped roasted hazelnuts

Place cream cheese in small bowl, soften on HIGH for 30 seconds. Add milk, vanilla and sifted icing sugar, beat until smooth. Place chocolate in small bowl, melt on HIGH for 1 minute. Fold chocolate into cream cheese with hazelnuts, spread into greased and lined 20cm square cake tin, refrigerate until set. Store in airtight container in refrigerator.

BUTTERSCOTCH BRAZIL NUTS
1 cup sugar
¼ cup water
½ cup liquid glucose
60g butter
100g brazil nut kernels

Combine sugar, water and glucose in deep 2 litre dish. Cook on HIGH 5 minutes, stirring occasionally until sugar is dissolved. Cook on HIGH 12 to 15 minutes, or until dark golden brown. To test if toffee is cooked, drop a teaspoon of syrup into a cup of cold water. It will set immediately then crack when snapped between fingers. Stir butter in quickly, then nuts. Using 2 teaspoons, spoon nuts onto greased oven trays. When set, store in airtight container.

CARAMEL POPCORN
¼ cup popping corn
¼ cup golden syrup
½ cup brown sugar, firmly packed
1 teaspoon vinegar
30g butter
½ cup shredded coconut

Place corn in deep ovenproof dish, cover with lid (not tight fitting), cook on HIGH 5 minutes. Combine golden syrup, brown sugar and vinegar in deep 2 litre dish, cook on HIGH 7 minutes or until dark golden brown. Mix in butter, popcorn and coconut, press into lightly greased 20cm square cake tin. Cut when cold, store in an airtight container.

CHOC GRAND MARNIER BALLS
½ cup raisins
½ cup sultanas
2 cups stale butter cake crumbs
½ cup coconut
¼ cup sugar
2 teaspoons grated orange rind
1 tablespoon orange juice
2 tablespoons Grand Marnier
15g butter
100g dark cooking chocolate, chopped
extra coconut

Chop raisins and sultanas finely, combine with cake crumbs, coconut, sugar and orange rind. Place orange juice, Grand Marnier, butter and chocolate in small bowl, melt on HIGH 1 minute, add to fruit mixture, mix well. Roll teaspoonfuls of mixture into balls, roll in extra coconut, refrigerate until firm.

Makes about 30.
Note: Cake crumbs can be made by combining half a 375g packet buttercake mix with ½ cup water, pour into greased pie plate, cook on HIGH 3 minutes.

Clockwise from top: Caramel Popcorn; Creamy Caramels; Choc Grand Marnier Balls; Cream Cheese Fudge; Almond Brittle; Butterscotch Brazil Nuts.

CHOCOLATE CARAMEL SLICE

2 x 60g Mars bars
75g unsalted butter
1 tablespoon golden syrup
3 cups Rice Bubbles
185g dark cooking chocolate,
    chopped

Place chopped Mars bars, butter and golden syrup in large bowl, melt on HIGH 2 to 3 minutes. Stir in Rice Bubbles, press over base of greased lamington tin (base measures 16cm x 26cm). Place chocolate in small bowl, melt on HIGH 1½ minutes, spread evenly over slice, refrigerate until set.

FRUITY LEMON SLICE

185g butter
¾ cup brown sugar, firmly packed
1 egg
1 teaspoon vanilla
1 cup (185g) chopped mixed fruit
½ cup chopped walnuts
1½ cups self-raising flour
1 teaspoon cinnamon
ICING
2 tablespoons lemon juice
1½ cups icing sugar
1 tablespoon coconut

Place butter in large bowl, melt on HIGH 1 minute. Mix in remaining ingredients. Spread mixture into greased 23cm round dish. Cook on HIGH 6 to 8 minutes or until just cooked in centre. Spread with Lemon Icing, sprinkle with coconut. Cool in dish, cut when cold.

Lemon icing: Heat lemon juice in a small bowl on HIGH 1 minute, beat in sifted icing sugar.

CHOCOLATE PECAN BROWNIES

100g dark cooking chocolate, chopped
90g butter
1 cup castor sugar
2 eggs
1 teaspoon vanilla
1 cup plain flour
1 tablespoon self-raising flour
½ cup chopped pecan nuts
CHOCOLATE ICING
100g dark cooking chocolate, chopped
¼ cup sour cream
½ cup pecan nuts

Combine chocolate and butter in large bowl, melt on HIGH 1 to 1½ minutes. Beat in sugar, eggs and vanilla then sifted flours and nuts. Pour into greased and lined 20cm round dish. Place dish on an upturned saucer, cook on HIGH 8 minutes or until just cooked in centre; stand 5 minutes. Turn onto wire rack to cool. Top with Chocolate Icing and nuts when cold.
Chocolate Icing: Place chocolate in small bowl, melt on HIGH 1 to 1½ minutes, stirring occasionally, stir in sour cream.

NUTTY MARSHMALLOW PATTIES

30g butter
2 tablespoons peanut butter
100g packet marshmallows
3 cups Rice Bubbles
½ cup roasted, unsalted peanuts
glace cherries

Place butter in large bowl, melt on HIGH 1 minute. Add peanut butter and marshmallows, cook on HIGH 30 seconds, or until marshmallows are melted. Stir in Rice Bubbles and peanuts, drop spoonfuls into paper patty cases, top with pieces of cherry, refrigerate.

Makes about 18.

CHOCOLATE CRUNCH SLICE

125g butter
1 cup self-raising flour
½ cup coconut
½ cup cornflakes
½ cup brown sugar
CHOCOLATE ICING
100g dark cooking chocolate, chopped
30g Copha, chopped

Place butter in large bowl, melt on HIGH 1 minute, stir in remaining ingredients, press into greased and lined 23cm square dish. Cook on HIGH 4 minutes or until just cooked in centre. Spread with Chocolate Icing, cut when cold.
Chocolate Icing: Place chocolate and Copha in small bowl, melt on HIGH 1½ minutes, stirring often.

OPPOSITE PAGE: Left, Chocolate Pecan Brownies; right, Chocolate Caramel Slice and Fruity Lemon Slice.
RIGHT: Left, Nutty Marshmallow Patties; right, Chocolate Crunch Slice.

DO-AHEAD DINNER PARTY

The food for this dinner party is light, delicious and enough for 6 people. Follow our instructions for do-ahead tips and order of cooking.

- *Cook Tomato Coulis the morning of the dinner party.*
- *Make the Cheesecake the day before the party.*
- *Make the stuffing for the Apricot Chicken, fill chicken fillets and pour over Lemon Mustard Sauce. Leave covered until cooking time.*
- *Cook Wild Rice and Broccoli in the afternoon. Pour over lemon juice and oil before serving.*
- *Prepare Zucchini Timbales and pour into souffle dishes. This can be done in the afternoon. When guests arrive, bake Timbales for 5 minutes on MEDIUM-LOW and turn out.*
- *Then bake Apricot Chicken 12 minutes on HIGH and serve.*
- *Wild Rice and Broccoli can be reheated; spread over base of shallow dish, cover, cook on HIGH 3 minutes.*

MENU

Zucchini Timbales with Tomato Coulis

Apricot Chicken with Lemon Mustard Sauce

Wild Rice with Broccoli

Chocolate Cream Cheesecake

ZUCCHINI TIMBALES WITH TOMATO COULIS

8 small (500g) zucchini
300g carton sour cream
2 tablespoons grated parmesan cheese
2 tablespoons chopped fresh basil
4 eggs
TOMATO COULIS
2 tomatoes, peeled, chopped
1 clove garlic, crushed
2 teaspoons tomato paste

Puree zucchini in blender or processor, place in bowl, cook on HIGH 5 minutes, drain well, pressing out as much liquid as possible, place in bowl. Stir in sour cream, parmesan cheese, basil and lightly beaten eggs. Divide mixture between 6 individual dishes (½ cup capacity), cover each dish; cook on MEDIUM 8 minutes. Turn onto serving plates, spoon Tomato Coulis around each one. Garnish with slice of zucchini and tomato if desired.
Tomato Coulis: Combine tomatoes, garlic and tomato paste in bowl, cook on HIGH 5 minutes, puree in blender or processor, strain.

RIGHT:
Apricot Chicken with Lemon Mustard Sauce and Wild Rice with Broccoli.

BELOW:
Zucchini Timbales with Tomato Coulis

APRICOT CHICKEN WITH LEMON MUSTARD SAUCE

4 chicken breast fillets
⅓ cup chopped dried apricots
2 tablespoons currants
30g butter
3 green shallots, chopped
1 clove garlic, crushed
1 stick celery, chopped
¾ cup stale breadcrumbs
1 tablespoon chopped chives
LEMON MUSTARD SAUCE
15g butter
1 cup chicken stock
1 teaspoon grainy mustard
2½ teaspoons cornflour
1 tablespoon lemon juice
⅓ cup cream

Cut a deep pocket in thickest part of each chicken fillet. Place apricots and currants in bowl, cover with hot water, cook on HIGH 2 minutes; drain well. Melt butter in bowl on HIGH 30 seconds, mix in fruit, shallots, garlic, celery and breadcrumbs.

Divide filling between chicken. Place chicken in dish in single layer, pour sauce over, cook on HIGH 12 minutes. Serve sprinkled with chives.
Lemon Mustard Sauce Combine butter, stock, mustard, blended cornflour and lemon juice and cream in bowl, cook on HIGH 3 minutes or until sauce boils and thickens. Stir once during cooking.

CHOCOLATE CREAM CHEESECAKE
60g butter
125g packaged plain un-iced
   chocolate biscuits, crushed
250g packet cream cheese
¼ cup sugar
2 eggs
60g dark cooking chocolate
300ml carton thickened cream
1 tablespoon Tia Maria

Melt butter in bowl on HIGH 1 minute, mix in biscuit crumbs. Press firmly over base and side of pie plate (base measures 18cm), cook on HIGH 1 minute, cool. Beat cream cheese and sugar in small bowl of electric mixer until smooth, add eggs one at a time, beat well. Melt chocolate in bowl on HIGH 1 minute, cool slightly, beat into cream cheese mixture with ½ cup of the cream and the Tia Maria. Pour into crumb crust, cook on MEDIUM HIGH 3 minutes, stand 5 minutes, cook on MEDIUM HIGH further 3 minutes or until just set. When cool, refrigerate several hours, spread with remaining whipped cream, decorate with strawberries and chocolate curls if desired.

WILD RICE WITH BROCCOLI
200g packet wild rice
2 cups water
125g broccoli
1 tablespoon water, extra
1 small red pepper, chopped
1 small stick celery, chopped
2 tablespoons chopped parsley
2 tablespoons lemon juice
2 tablespoons oil

Combine rice and water in bowl, cover, cook on HIGH 25 minutes; stand 5 minutes. Cut broccoli into flowerets, place in bowl with extra water, cover, cook on HIGH 3 minutes; drain. Add pepper, celery and parsley, combine with rice. Mix in combined lemon juice and oil.

A QUICK-AND-EASY DINNER PARTY FOR SIX

This dinner party takes little time to prepare and we've included some helpful steps for boning out the lamb. Here is a suggested order of work:

- *Butterfly lamb, following pictures below, and marinate.*
- *Make soup during the day of the dinner party.*
- *Parboil vegetables and rinse under cold water; drain.*
- *Make Sour Cream Cherry Cake in the afternoon of the dinner party.*
- *When guests arrive, reheat soup 8 minutes on HIGH.*
- *Cook lamb as soon as soup is served (it takes 20 minutes on HIGH).*
- *Make sauce, strain and serve in sauce boat.*
- *While carving lamb, cook vegetables in savory butter 3 minutes on HIGH.*

STEP 1: Use sharp knife to cut down and around bone.

STEP 2: Scrape away as much meat from bone as possible; remove bone.

STEP 3: Cut down (without cutting through) into thickest part of meat, so that meat can be opened out flat.

MENU

Creamy Asparagus Soup

Orange and Ginger Butterflied Lamb

Carrot and Zucchini Julienne

Sour Cream Cherry Cake

SOUR CREAM CHERRY CAKE

125g butter
½ packet Buttercake Mix
½ cup coconut
1 egg
2 x 410g cans pitted black cherries, drained
1 cup sour cream
2 tablespoons sugar
1 egg, extra
½ teaspoon cinnamon

Melt butter in pie plate (base measures 18cm) on HIGH 1 minute. Add dry cake mix, coconut and egg, mix with fork until combined, spread over base of pie plate, cook on HIGH 4 minutes. Top with well drained cherries. Mix sour cream with sugar and extra egg, spoon over cherries, cook on HIGH 5 minutes or until set. Sprinkle with cinnamon, serve hot or cold with whipped cream.

CREAMY ASPARAGUS SOUP

1 bundle (250g) fresh asparagus
2 tablespoons water
1 onion, finely chopped
1 stick celery, finely chopped
15g butter
1 cup chicken stock
2 x 340g cans green asparagus spears
¼ cup dry vermouth
300ml carton thickened cream

Place asparagus in shallow dish, add water, cover, cook on HIGH 3 minutes or until just tender, drain and chop. Combine onion, celery and butter in bowl, cook on HIGH 3 minutes. Add stock and undrained cans of asparagus, cook on HIGH 5 minutes. Puree mixture in processor or blender until smooth, place in bowl, stir in vermouth, cream and chopped asparagus. Cook on HIGH 3 minutes or until heated through.

92

ORANGE AND GINGER BUTTERFLIED LAMB

1.5kg leg lamb
1 onion, chopped
1 teaspoon grated fresh ginger
1 clove garlic, crushed
½ cup orange juice
½ cup orange marmalade
½ cup white vinegar
3 teaspoons cornflour
2 teaspoons water
1 teaspoon soy sauce

Ask butcher to bone out lamb. Remove skin and fat from lamb, cut lamb so that it sits flat. Combine onion, ginger, garlic, orange juice, marmalade and vinegar in shallow dish, add lamb, cover, marinate several hours, turning occasionally, or refrigerate overnight.

Drain lamb; reserve marinade. Place lamb in shallow dish, cover, cook on HIGH 20 minutes. Remove lamb, cover to keep warm. Add marinade to juices in dish, stir in blended cornflour, water and soy sauce, cook on HIGH 4 minutes or until sauce boils and thickens; stir after 2 minutes. Strain sauce, serve with sliced lamb.

CARROT AND ZUCCHINI JULIENNE

3 carrots
2 zucchini
1 tablespoon water
60g mushrooms, thinly sliced
60g butter
2 tablespoons chopped parsley
1 clove garlic, crushed
2 teaspoons canned green peppercorns, drained

Cut carrots and zucchini into thin strips about 5cm in length. Place carrots in bowl, add water, cover, cook on HIGH 3 minutes, add zucchini and mushrooms. Add butter, parsley, garlic and peppercorns to vegetables, cook on HIGH 3 minutes.

CONVECTION/MICROWAVE COOKING

Cooking in a CONVECTION/MICROWAVE oven gives you the best of both worlds. The CONVECTION part of the oven is just another oven in the kitchen. However, it has the unique advantage of being able to work in conjunction with the MICROWAVE part of the oven. Some foods — such as pastries — respond best to CONVECTION, then, once they are partly cooked and filling has been added, the overall cooking time can be reduced by introducing the MICROWAVE part of the oven.
We didn't find it necessary to use special dishes or cake tins when using the CONVECTION/MICROWAVE combination. The easy rule to remember is that about two-thirds of the surface of a metal container must be covered with food. Also — as with any oven used for baking — it is best to use a rack so that the food is elevated slightly and tends to be toward the centre and upper half of the oven. Another helpful tip — round or oval dishes will give better results than square or rectangular. If you haven't any choice, use pieces of aluminium foil to cover the corners of the dish (see page 4) after food appears to be cooked. It is not necessary to preheat the oven unless cooking foods such as biscuits, some pastries, etc., which have short cooking times. Individual recipes state when necessary.

CAKES, BISCUITS, AND SLICES ETC.

All the recipes in this section have been cooked using the CONVECTION/MICROWAVE method. Any of your favorite cake or biscuit recipes can be cooked this way; experiment and note reductions in cooking time for future reference.

It is quite safe to use metal cake pans and, of course, microwaveproof pans. As with conventional cooking methods, times given in recipes are only a guide. Times will vary depending on type of oven, type of cooking container, temperature of ingredients, the absorbency rate of flour and accuracy in measuring ingredients.

As a guide, tend to undercook cakes (as for microwave cooking); they should feel JUST set in the middle because they continue to cook and dry out a little more out of the oven. If in doubt, test with a skewer slightly away from centre.

All cakes and biscuits give best results when cooked on the low rack in the microwave oven so the food (like a conventional oven) is roughly in the centre and upper half of the oven. However, if two trays of biscuits or patty cakes are being cooked at the same time, place them on the upper and lower rack and change their positions around halfway during cooking. These recipes indicate when to use an electric mixer; processors will not give the same results.

Note that some recipes tell you to preheat the oven; this mostly applies to food which takes only a short time to cook.

ORANGE MARMALADE CAKE

185g butter
2 teaspoons grated orange rind
¾ cup sugar
3 eggs, separated
½ cup marmalade
⅓ cup mixed peel
2½ cups self-raising flour
½ cup milk
¼ cup orange juice
ORANGE FROSTING
60g butter
2 teaspoons grated orange rind
1 cup icing sugar
1 tablespoon orange juice

Cream butter, orange rind, sugar and egg yolks in small bowl of electric mixer until light and fluffy. Stir in marmalade and peel, then sifted flour alternately with milk and orange juice. Beat egg whites until firm peaks form, fold gently into cake mixture. Pour into greased and lined deep 20cm square cake tin, bake on CONVECTION/MICROWAVE 150°C for 35 minutes. Turn onto wire rack to cool. Spread with Frosting.

Orange Frosting: Cream butter and orange rind, gradually beat in sifted icing sugar and orange juice.

Back from left: Pineapple Butter Cake; Sour Cream Lemon Syrup Cake. Front from left: Sour Cream Apple Cake; Orange Marmalade Cake; Chocolate Orange Cake.

PINEAPPLE BUTTER CAKE
450g can pineapple pieces
185g butter
½ cup milk
½ cup castor sugar
½ teaspoon bicarbonate soda
2 eggs
2¼ cups self-raising flour

Drain pineapple, reserve ½ cup syrup. Combine butter, milk, reserved pineapple syrup, pineapple and sugar in bowl, cook on HIGH 5 minutes, stir in soda, stand 5 minutes. Stir in lightly beaten eggs and sifted flour. Pour mixture into greased 20cm ring tin; cook on CONVECTION/MICROWAVE 180°C for 25 minutes. Cool in tin 5 minutes, turn onto wire rack to cool. If desired, decorate with whipped cream, pineapple and shredded coconut.

SOUR CREAM APPLE CAKE
125g butter
1 teaspoon vanilla
¾ cup castor sugar
2 eggs
½ cup sour cream
1 cup self-raising flour
½ cup plain flour
410g can pie apple
1 tablespoon brown sugar
½ teaspoon cinnamon

Cream butter, vanilla, castor sugar and eggs in small basin of electric mixer until light and fluffy. Stir in sour cream and sifted flours. Spread half the mixture into greased and base-lined 20cm ring tin, top evenly with half the combined apples, brown sugar and cinnamon. Spread with remaining cake mixture, then remaining apple mixture. Cook on CONVECTION/MICROWAVE 180°C for 40 minutes. Stand 10 minutes, before turning onto wire rack; invert.

SOUR CREAM LEMON SYRUP CAKE
250g butter
1 tablespoon grated lemon rind
1¼ cups castor sugar
3 eggs
¾ cup sour cream
1 cup self-raising flour
½ cup plain flour
LEMON SYRUP
⅓ cup lemon juice
¼ cup sugar

Cream butter, lemon rind and sugar until light and fluffy, beat in eggs one at a time. Stir in sour cream, then sifted flours; mix until smooth. Pour into greased 20cm ring or baba tin; cook on CONVECTION/MICROWAVE 180°C for 25 minutes. Cool in tin 5 minutes, turn onto wire rack with tray underneath. Pour hot syrup evenly over hot cake.

Lemon Syrup: Combine lemon juice and sugar in pan, stir over heat until sugar has dissolved; bring to boil.

CHOCOLATE ORANGE CAKE
60g dark cooking chocolate, chopped
60g butter
¼ cup water
1½ cups self-raising flour
2 tablespoons cocoa
1 cup castor sugar
1 egg
2 teaspoons grated orange rind
¼ cup orange juice
¼ cup milk
CHOCOLATE ICING
1½ cups icing sugar
2 tablespoons cocoa
1 teaspoon soft butter
2 tablespoons orange juice, approximately

Combine chocolate, butter and water in bowl, cook on HIGH 1 minute, stir until melted. Stir in sifted flour and cocoa, sugar, lightly beaten egg, orange rind, orange juice and milk; stir until smooth. Pour into greased and base-lined deep 20cm round cake tin; cook on CONVECTION/MICROWAVE 180°C for 20 minutes. Cool in tin 5 minutes before turning onto wire rack to cool. When cold top with Chocolate Icing.

Chocolate Icing: Sift icing sugar and cocoa into bowl, stir in butter and enough orange juice to give a stiff paste. Stir over hot water until smooth and spreadable.

CHOCOLATE NUT AND CHERRY SLICE

Use nuts of your choice for this recipe.

125g butter
1 teaspoon grated lemon rind
½ cup sugar
1 egg
½ cup chopped nuts
¼ cup chopped glace cherries
1¼ cups self-raising flour
200g dark cooking chocolate, chopped

Cream butter, lemon rind and sugar on electric mixer until light and fluffy, beat in egg. Fold in nuts and cherries; then sifted flour. Spread mixture evenly into well greased lamington tin (base measures 16cm x 26cm); cook on CONVECTION/MICROWAVE 180°C for 15 minutes; cool in tin. Melt chocolate over hot water, spread evenly on top. Refrigerate until set before cutting.

SULTANA CORNFLAKE COOKIES

If cooking 2 trays at once, change shelf positions after 6 minutes.

125g butter
½ cup castor sugar
1 egg
½ cup sultanas
½ cup coconut
1 cup self-raising flour
2 cups cornflakes, lightly crushed

Cream butter, sugar and egg on electric mixer until light and fluffy. Stir in sultanas, coconut and sifted flour. Roll teaspoonfuls of mixture into balls, roll in cornflakes, place on lightly greased oven trays 2cm apart. Preheat oven to 180°C, bake on CONVECTION/MICROWAVE 180°C for 8 minutes or until lightly browned. Place on wire rack to cool.

Makes about 24.

CHOCOLATE GINGER BISCUITS

If cooking 2 trays at once, change shelf positions after 4 minutes.

125g butter
¾ cup brown sugar, lightly packed
1 egg
1¾ cups self-raising flour
¼ cup cocoa
¾ cup (125g) finely chopped glace ginger
30g dark cooking chocolate

Cream butter and sugar on electric mixer until light and fluffy, add egg, beat well. Stir in sifted flour and cocoa, then ginger. Shape teaspoonfuls of mixture into balls, place on lightly greased oven trays, allow room for spreading. Cook on CONVECTION/MICROWAVE 180°C for 8 minutes, cool on trays. Drizzle with melted chocolate.

Makes about 40.

PROCESSOR CHOCOLATE NUT BROWNIES

½ cup roasted hazelnuts
⅔ cup plain flour
60g dark cooking chocolate, chopped
1 cup castor sugar
125g butter
1 tablespoon rum
1 teaspoon vanilla
2 eggs
200g dark cooking chocolate, chopped, extra
¼ cup cream

Back: Peanut Butter Cheesecake Slice; Chocolate Nut and Cherry Slice. Front from left: Processor Chocolate Nut Brownies; Sultana Cornflake Cookies; Chocolate Ginger Biscuits.

Process hazelnuts and flour until finely ground, remove. Process chocolate and sugar until chocolate is finely ground. Add chopped butter gradually while processor is operating, process until combined. Add rum, then eggs one at a time, when combined add hazelnut mixture. Pour into greased and lined 23cm square cake tin. Bake on CONVECTION/MICROWAVE 180°C for 20 minutes, cool 10 minutes, turn onto wire rack to cool.

Combine extra chocolate and cream in bowl, cook on HIGH 1 minute, beat until smooth, cool to room temperature before spreading over top and sides of brownie. Refrigerate until set before cutting.

PEANUT BUTTER CHEESECAKE SLICE

30g butter
½ cup crunchy peanut butter
¼ cup sugar
1 egg
1 cup self-raising flour
½ cup strawberry jam
250g packet cream cheese
¼ cup sugar, extra
1 egg, extra

Place butter and peanut butter in bowl, cook on HIGH 1 minute or until butter is melted. Stir in sugar, egg and sifted flour, press over base of 23cm flan tin. Cook on CONVECTION/MICROWAVE 180°C for 10 minutes, cool 10 minutes. Spread with jam. Beat softened cream cheese, extra sugar and extra egg together until smooth. Pour over jam, cook on CONVECTION/MICROWAVE 180°C for 10 minutes, cool in tin, cut when cold.

PEANUT BUTTER AND CHOCOLATE COOKIES

An assortment of cookies can be made from this one recipe. The handy part is, the mixture can be made ahead, wrapped and frozen for up to 2 weeks, then cut off the roll, cooked and served oven fresh.

125g dark cooking chocolate,
**   chopped**
250g butter
1 cup crunchy peanut butter
1½ cups brown sugar, lightly
**   packed**
2 eggs
1½ cups self-raising flour
½ cup plain flour
1½ cups rolled oats
½ cup roasted unsalted peanuts,
**   finely chopped**

Melt chocolate in small bowl on HIGH 1 minute, cool to lukewarm. Cream butter, peanut butter and sugar on electric mixer until light and fluffy, beat in eggs, fold in sifted flours and rolled oats. Divide mixture into two bowls, stir chocolate into one half of the mixture. Cover, refrigerate both bowls of mixture for 1 hour.

STEP 1: Roll half the peanut butter mixture between two pieces of lightly floured plastic food wrap into a rectangle measuring about 24cm x 32cm. Repeat with half of the chocolate mixture. Remove the two top pieces of plastic food wrap. Place the chocolate rectangle directly on top of the peanut butter rectangle, trim edges neatly.

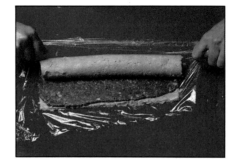

STEP 2: Roll up like a swiss roll, using the plastic food wrap to help. Coat roll in peanuts. Cover with plastic food wrap, refrigerate several hours or freeze for up to two weeks.

STEP 3: Preheat oven to 180°C. Cut rolls into 5mm slices. Place 3cm apart on lightly greased oven trays, bake on CONVECTION/MICROWAVE 180°C for 10 minutes or until firm. Cool on wire rack.
Shape remaining dough into rolls about 5cm in diameter, cover with plastic food wrap and freeze, or roll dough out to 3mm thickness between lightly floured plastic food wrap. Cut into 6cm rounds, bake as above. If desired, dip edges of cookies in melted chocolate, or sandwich cookies with melted chocolate, allow to set on wire rack at room temperature.
Makes about 60 cookies.

BANANA CINNAMON TEACAKE

4 ripe bananas
⅓ cup brown sugar
⅓ cup water
60g butter
½ cup castor sugar
1 egg
1 cup self-raising flour
1 teaspoon cinnamon
⅓ cup milk

Slice two of the bananas. Combine brown sugar and water in bowl, cook on HIGH 3 minutes, add sliced bananas, cook on HIGH 2 minutes, drain, reserve syrup.

Cream butter, sugar and egg together in electric mixer. Stir in sifted flour and cinnamon, then milk. Pour half the cake mixture into greased and lined 20cm recess tin, top with cooked sliced bananas, spread with remaining cake mixture. Cook on CONVECTION/MICROWAVE 180°C for 20 minutes. Stand 5 minutes, turn onto serving plate. Fill recess with remaining sliced bananas. Cook reserved syrup on HIGH 2 minutes, brush hot syrup over top and side of cake, serve cake warm.

UPSIDE DOWN DATE AND WALNUT CAKE

⅓ cup chopped dates
¼ cup brown sugar
1 tablespoon custard powder
¼ cup milk
1 egg
¼ cup chopped walnuts
125g butter
1 teaspoon vanilla
¾ cup castor sugar
2 eggs, extra
½ cup self-raising flour
¼ cup milk

Combine dates, brown sugar and custard powder in bowl; stir in milk, cook on HIGH 2 minutes, beat well, cool. Stir in beaten egg and walnuts. Spread evenly over base of greased base lined 20cm ring tin.

Cream butter, vanilla, castor sugar and extra eggs in electric mixer until light and fluffy. Stir in sifted flour and milk. Spread cake mixture over date and walnut mixture. Cook on rack on CONVECTION/MICROWAVE 150°C for 20 minutes, cool in tin 5 minutes, turn onto serving plate, serve warm.

Peanut Butter and Chocolate Cookies

FRUIT AND BRAN LOAF

This loaf should be served with butter on the day it is made.

300ml carton cream
2 teaspoons lemon juice
2 eggs
60g butter, melted
¾ cup (125g) chopped dates
1½ cups packaged Sultana Bran
½ cup finely chopped dried
   apricots
½ cup sultanas
1 cup brown sugar, lightly packed
2 cups wholemeal self-raising flour

Blend or process combined cream, lemon juice, eggs, butter and dates until dates are finely chopped. Combine date mixture with Sultana Bran, apricots, sultanas and sugar, stir in sifted flour. Spread mixture into lightly greased base-lined loaf tin (base measures 12cm x 22cm). Bake on CONVECTION/MICROWAVE 180°C for 30 minutes.

ABOVE:
Back from left: Fruit and Bran Loaf;
Banana Pecan Muffins. Front from left:
Upside Down Date and Walnut Cake;
Banana Cinnamon Teacake.

BANANA PECAN MUFFINS

1 cup wholemeal plain flour
½ cup wholemeal self-raising flour
1 teaspoon bicarbonate of soda
1½ cups unprocessed bran
¾ cup raw sugar
½ cup chopped pecan nuts
2 large very ripe bananas, mashed
125g butter, melted
1 egg
1 cup buttermilk

BRANDIED CHOCOLATE NUT TORTE

4 eggs, separated
¾ cup castor sugar
2 teaspoons grated orange rind
2 tablespoons orange juice
2 tablespoons brandy
1 tablespoon plain flour
¾ cup (125g) finely chopped pecan nuts
100g dark cooking chocolate, grated

TOPPING
300ml carton thickened cream
1 tablespoon brandy

Beat egg yolks, sugar, orange rind, orange juice and brandy until thick and creamy, fold in sifted flour. Beat egg whites until firm peaks form, gently fold ⅓ of the egg whites into egg yolk mixture, then nuts and chocolate, then remaining egg whites. Pour mixture into greased and base-lined deep 23cm round cake tin; cook on CONVECTION/MICROWAVE 150°C for 20 minutes. Cool in tin 5 minutes, turn onto wire rack. Cover cake with Topping. If desired, decorate with orange slices, extra grated chocolate and extra chopped nuts.

Topping: Beat cream and brandy until thick.

HONEY SPICE CAKE WITH COFFEE ICING

½ cup hot water
½ teaspoon instant coffee powder
2 eggs, separated
⅓ cup castor sugar
90g butter, melted
½ cup honey
1½ cups self-raising flour
½ teaspoon mixed spice

COFFEE ICING
2 teaspoons instant coffee powder
2 tablespoons hot milk
2 cups icing sugar
15g butter
¼ cup finely chopped walnuts

Dissolve coffee in hot water, cool. Beat egg yolks and sugar on electric mixer until thick, beat in cool butter and honey. Stir in sifted flour and spice alternately with cold coffee mixture. Beat egg whites until firm peaks form, fold gently into cake mixture, pour into greased base-lined 20cm ring tin. Cook on CONVECTION/MICROWAVE 180°C for 20 minutes. Turn out, stand 5 minutes, spread with Coffee Icing, sprinkle with walnuts.

Coffee Icing: Dissolve coffee in milk, stir into sifted icing sugar with soft butter, beat until smooth and spreadable.

Sift flours and soda into basin, mix in bran, sugar and pecans. Combine bananas, butter, lightly beaten egg and buttermilk, pour into well in centre of dry ingredients, mix with fork until just combined. Drop tablespoonfuls of mixture into greased muffin tins, cook on CONVECTION/MICROWAVE 180°C for 15 minutes.

Makes about 18 muffins.

RIGHT:
Brandied Chocolate Nut Torte

CHOCOLATE CARROT CAKE
1 cup self-raising flour
2 tablespoons cocoa
½ teaspoon bicarbonate of soda
½ cup castor sugar
1 Granny Smith apple, finely grated
2 eggs
¾ cup (125g) chopped pecan nuts
1 cup finely grated carrot
½ cup oil
CREAM CHEESE FROSTING
60g packaged cream cheese
45g butter
2 cups icing sugar
2 teaspoons rum

Sift flour, cocoa, soda and sugar into bowl. Add apple, lightly beaten eggs, pecans, carrot and oil, mix well. Pour into greased and lined deep 20cm cake tin, cook on CONVECTION/MICROWAVE 180°C for 25 minutes. Stand 5 minutes, turn onto wire rack to cool. If desired, cover with Frosting and decorate with extra pecan nuts.

Cream Cheese Frosting: Beat soft cream cheese and butter together until smooth, gradually beat in sifted icing sugar and rum.

102

OATY DATE AND WALNUT CAKE
185g butter
1½ cups brown sugar, lightly packed
2 eggs
1 cup self-raising flour
½ teaspoon cinnamon
1 cup rolled oats
¾ cup (125g) chopped dates
½ cup chopped walnuts
½ cup water

Beat butter, sugar and eggs together on electric mixer until light and fluffy. Stir in sifted flour and cinnamon, oats, dates, walnuts and water. Spread evenly into base-lined greased 20cm ring tin. Bake on CONVECTION/MICROWAVE 180°C for 30 minutes. Serve buttered.

Back: Chocolate Carrot Cake. Centre from left: Honey Spice Cake with Coffee Icing; Oaty Date and Walnut Cake. Front: Hot Caramel Banana Cake.

HOT CARAMEL BANANA CAKE
60g butter
1 cup brown sugar, firmly packed
⅓ cup buttermilk
2 cups self-raising flour
1½ cups castor sugar
125g butter, softened, extra
½ cup coconut
2 eggs
1 cup buttermilk, extra
2 large ripe bananas, mashed
2 tablespoon coconut, extra

Combine butter, brown sugar and buttermilk in small bowl, cook on HIGH 2 minutes, set aside. Combine flour, sugar, butter, coconut, eggs, extra buttermilk and bananas in bowl of electric mixer, beat until well combined. Pour into greased and lined 23cm square tin. Bake on CONVECTION/MICROWAVE 150°C for 40 minutes. Pour over reserved caramel mixture, sprinkle with extra coconut, bake further 5 minutes; stand 10 minutes before turning out, serve warm.

QUICK MIX FRUIT CAKE

1kg mixed fruit
⅓ cup brandy
1 tablespoon honey
¾ cup brown sugar, firmly packed
3 eggs
185g butter, melted
1 cup plain flour
½ cup self-raising flour
1 teaspoon mixed spice
2 tablespoons brandy, extra

Combine fruit, brandy, honey, brown sugar and lightly beaten eggs in bowl. Stir in cooled butter, then sifted flours and spice. Spread into greased and lined deep 20cm round cake tin, cook on CONVECTION/MICROWAVE 150°C for 50 minutes. Brush with extra brandy, cover, cool in tin.

Back from left: Rich Fruit Cake; Quick Mix Fruit Cake. Front from left: Boiled Rum and Raisin Cake; Cream Cheese Cherry Cake.

BOILED RUM AND RAISIN CAKE

500g raisins
1½ cups (250g) finely chopped dried apricots
90g butter
½ cup brown sugar, firmly packed
½ teaspoon cinnamon
⅓ cup water
½ cup rum
1 egg
2 tablespoons apricot jam
¾ cup self-raising flour
¾ cup plain flour
2 tablespoons rum, extra

Combine raisins, apricots, butter, sugar, cinnamon, water and rum in large bowl. Cook on HIGH 7 minutes; allow mixture to become completely cold. Stir in lightly beaten egg, jam and sifted flours. Spread into greased and base-lined 20cm ring tin, cook in CONVECTION/MICROWAVE 150°C for 30 minutes. Brush with extra rum, cool in tin.

CREAM CHEESE CHERRY CAKE

125g glace cherries
125g butter
2 teaspoons grated lemon rind
125g packet cream cheese
1 cup castor sugar
3 eggs
¾ cup plain flour
¾ cup self-raising flour
¾ cup (125g) sultanas

Halve about 6 glace cherries for decorating, quarter remaining cherries. Cream butter, lemon rind, cream cheese and sugar on electric mixer until light and fluffy. Add eggs one at a time, beating well after each addition. Fold in sifted flours, sultanas and quartered cherries. Spread mixture into greased and lined deep 20cm round cake tin, decorate with halved cherries. Cook on CONVECTION/MICROWAVE 150°C for 40 minutes. Stand 5 minutes before turning onto wire rack to cool.

RICH FRUIT CAKE

1½ cups (250g) sultanas
¾ cup currants
⅓ cup chopped raisins
⅓ cup chopped glace cherries
⅓ cup mixed peel
¼ cup brandy
125g butter
¾ cup black sugar, firmly packed
2 eggs
1 tablespoon marmalade
2 teaspoons parisian essence
1½ cups plain flour
1 teaspoon mixed spice
2 tablespoons brandy, extra

Combine fruit in large basin with brandy. Cover, stand overnight or up to a week.

Line a deep 15cm square cake tin with 2 thicknesses of greaseproof paper. Beat butter until soft, add sugar; beat only until combined. Add eggs one at a time, beating well after each addition. Stir in marmalade, parisian essence, then sifted dry ingredients. Spread evenly into tin, cook on CONVECTION/MICROWAVE 150°C for 35 minutes. While hot, brush evenly with extra brandy. Cover tightly with aluminium foil; leave until cold. Remove foil and tin, leave lining paper intact. Store in plastic food wrap in cool, dark place.

Both of these recipes are delicious and will make about 24 cakes. Aluminium patty pans can be used or the special microwaveproof patty pans.

FLUFFY PATTY CAKES

125g butter
½ cup castor sugar
1 teaspoon vanilla
2 eggs
½ cup milk
1½ cups self-raising flour
½ cup custard powder

Cream butter, sugar and vanilla until light and fluffy. Beat in eggs one at a time, add milk alternately with sifted flour and custard powder. Spoon into greased patty pans or paper patty cases. Preheat oven on 180°C, cook on CONVECTION/MICROWAVE 180°C for 10 minutes; cool on wire rack before icing.

QUICK MIX PATTY CAKES

½ cup custard powder
1½ cups self-raising flour
¾ cup castor sugar
125g butter, softened
3 eggs
¼ cup milk
1 teaspoon vanilla

Combine all ingredients in small bowl of electric mixer. Beat on medium speed 3 minutes or until mixture is smooth and changed in color. Drop teaspoonfuls of mixture into greased patty pans or paper patty cases. Preheat oven to 180°C, cook on CONVECTION/MICROWAVE 180°C for 10 minutes; cool on wire rack.

VARIATIONS

ICED Combine 1½ cups sifted icing sugar with 2 teaspoons soft butter, stir in about 1 tablespoon hot water to give a spreadable consistency. Color if desired or for Chocolate Icing; stir in 2 tablespoons sifted cocoa (a little more water will be necessary), spread onto cold cakes, sprinkle with hundreds and thousands, chopped nuts, coconut etc. before icing is set.

SNOWBALLS Bake cakes in shallow round-based patty pans. When cold, split cakes in half horizontally, fill with whipped cream, replace tops. Spread cakes all over with Chocolate Icing (see above), roll cakes in coconut before icing is set.

CHOCOLATE Sift ¼ cup cocoa with other dry ingredients, add to mixture, top with Chocolate Icing (see above).

SULTANA Stir ½ cup sultanas and 1 teaspoon cinnamon into cake mixture.

COFFEE Dissolve 1½ tablespoons coffee powder in 3 tablespoons hot water, add to cake mixture.

CINNAMON APPLE Add 1 teaspoon cinnamon to dry ingredients of cake mixture, spoon half mixture into 24 patty pans, top with a teaspoonful of canned pie apple, top with remaining cake mixture. These might take a minute or two longer to cook than other variations.

BUTTERFLY CAKES Cut circles from top of each cake, cut circles in half. Fill cakes with whipped cream, press "wings" into cream, dust with icing sugar, dot with a little jam if desired.

PASTRY

Pastry can be cooked successfully in the CONVECTION oven, then when teamed with a filling the cooking can be continued using either CONVECTION or CONVECTION/MICROWAVE. Follow individual recipes for directions. Preheat only when recipe specifies. Cooking on a rack, as you would in a conventional oven, will give best results.

MINI CHICKEN AND MUSHROOM PIES

4 chicken breast fillets
60g butter
2 bacon rashers, chopped
1 large onion, chopped
250g small mushrooms
¼ cup plain flour
1 cup milk
1 chicken stock cube
⅓ cup dry sherry
1 clove garlic, crushed
¼ cup chopped parsley
2 sheets Ready Rolled Puff Pastry
1 egg

Back from left: Mini Chicken and Mushroom Pies; Golden Cheese and Ham Puff. Front: Cream-Topped Steak and Mushroom Pie.

Cut chicken into bite-sized pieces. Combine butter, bacon, onion and mushrooms in large bowl, cook on HIGH 10 minutes, stir in flour, then milk, crumbled stock cube, sherry and garlic; cook on HIGH 3 minutes, add chicken, cook on HIGH 5 minutes, stir in parsley. Divide mixture between 4 dishes (1-cup capacity). Place a 1cm strip of pastry around rim of each dish, brush with a little water. Cut 4 circles of pastry 1cm larger than diameter of dish; place circles of pastry on top of dishes, seal edges. Brush with beaten egg, cut hole in top to allow steam to escape. Cook in preheated CONVECTION oven 220°C for 15 minutes or until golden brown.
Serves 4.

CREAM-TOPPED STEAK AND MUSHROOM PIE

PASTRY
1¾ cups plain flour
125g butter
1 teaspoon lemon juice
¼ cup water, approximately

FILLING
500g minced steak
1 large onion, finely chopped
30g butter
¼ cup tomato sauce
¼ teaspoon dried oregano leaves
½ x 53g packet mushroom soup
¾ cup boiling water
3 eggs
300g carton sour cream
½ cup milk
1 cup grated tasty cheese

Pastry: Sift flour into bowl, rub in butter, add lemon juice and enough water to mix to a firm dough. Roll dough large enough to cover base and side of 23cm springform tin, taking pastry 4cm up side of tin. Cover pastry with greaseproof paper, cover paper thickly with beans or rice. Cook in preheated CONVECTION oven 220°C for 10 minutes, remove paper and beans, bake further 5 minutes. Spread Filling over pastry, top with sour cream mixture, sprinkle with cheese, bake on CONVECTION/MICROWAVE 180°C for 20 minutes or until set and lightly browned. Stand 10 minutes before serving.

Filling: Cook onion and butter in bowl on HIGH 4 minutes, add mince, tomato sauce and oregano, cook on HIGH 5 minutes, stirring occasionally. Add soup mix and boiling water, cook on HIGH 15 minutes or until thick; cool. Beat eggs, sour cream and milk together.

GOLDEN CHEESE AND HAM PUFF

CHOUX PASTRY
1 cup boiling water
60g butter
1 cup plain flour
4 eggs
¾ cup grated swiss cheese

FILLING
30g butter
125g mushrooms, sliced
2 tablespoons plain flour
2 tablespoons dry sherry
½ cup chicken stock
½ cup cream
1 teaspoon grainy mustard
250g ham, chopped
4 green shallots, chopped
½ cup grated tasty cheese
1 tomato, sliced
¼ teaspoon dried basil leaves
1 tablespoon grated parmesan cheese

Combine water and butter in large bowl, cook on HIGH 3 minutes or until water is boiling. Add sifted flour all at once, stir until mixture forms a ball. Transfer to bowl of food processor. Add eggs one at a time while processor is operating, add cheese, continue processing until mixture is smooth and glossy. Spread around side of round or oval greased ovenproof dish (2.5 litre fluid capacity). Place Filling into centre, top with tomato, sprinkle with combined basil and parmesan cheese, bake in preheated CONVECTION oven 220°C for 15 minutes, change to CONVECTION/MICROWAVE 180°C, bake further 20 minutes or until pastry is puffed and golden brown.

Filling: Cook butter and mushrooms in bowl on HIGH 3 minutes, stir in flour, sherry, stock, cream and mustard, cook on HIGH 3 minutes or until mixture boils and thickens, stir in ham, shallots and tasty cheese.

Serves 4.

SAUSAGE AND ZUCCHINI FLAN

PASTRY
1½ cups plain flour
125g butter
2 tablespoons water, approximately

FILLING
200g (about 5) thin sausages
30g butter
1 onion, finely chopped
2 zucchini, sliced
2 tablespoons plain flour
1 teaspoon dry mustard
1 cup milk
2 eggs, separated
½ cup grated tasty cheese

Back: Sausage and Zucchini Flan. Left: Seafood Flan with Lemon Sauce.

Pastry: Sift flour into bowl, rub in butter, add enough water to mix to a firm dough. Roll dough large enough to cover side and base of 23cm flan tin, cover pastry with greaseproof paper, cover paper thickly with beans or rice. Bake in preheated CONVECTION oven 220°C for 10 minutes, remove beans and paper, bake further 5 minutes or until brown. Add Filling, cook on CONVECTION 200°C for 20 minutes or until set and golden brown.

Filling: Place sausages in single layer in shallow dish, bake on CONVECTION/MICROWAVE 180°C for 10 minutes or until cooked, slice sausages thinly. Cook butter, onion and zucchini in bowl on HIGH 5 minutes or until tender, stir in flour and mustard, cook on HIGH 1 minute. Blend in milk, cook on HIGH 3 minutes or until mixture boils and thickens, stir during cooking. Stir in egg yolks, cheese and sausages. Beat egg whites until firm, fold into sausage mixture.

SEAFOOD FLAN WITH LEMON SAUCE

500g green king prawns, shelled
440g can red salmon, drained
2 eggs
¾ cup cream
125g butter
6 sheets fillo pastry
LEMON SAUCE
30g butter
2 tablespoons lemon juice
1 cup chicken stock
½ cup cream
1 tablespoon cornflour
2 green shallots, chopped

Process prawns and salmon until smooth, add eggs and cream gradually while motor is operating. Melt butter in bowl on HIGH 1 minute, brush between layers of pastry. Place pastry into 20cm flan tin, trim edges. Add prawn filling, cook on CONVECTION/MICROWAVE 180°C for 20 minutes. Stand 5 minutes before cutting.

Lemon Sauce: Combine butter, lemon juice and stock in bowl, cook on HIGH 2 minutes. Stir in blended cornflour and cream, cook on HIGH 2 minutes or until sauce boils and thickens, stirring once; add shallots.

WALNUT AND ORANGE CREAM CHEESE FLAN

PASTRY
⅓ cup walnuts
1¼ cups plain flour
2 tablespoons castor sugar
90g butter
2 egg yolks
ORANGE CUSTARD
3 egg yolks
½ cup sugar
1½ tablespoons cornflour
¼ cup Grand Marnier
¾ cup milk
375g packaged cream cheese
3 teaspoons grated orange rind
TOPPING
4 oranges
¼ cup sugar
1 tablespoon Grand Marnier

Pastry: Process or blend walnuts until finely ground, add flour, sugar, then cold chopped butter, process until mixture is fine. Add egg yolks, process until pastry forms a ball. Turn onto lightly floured surface, knead lightly until smooth, cover, refrigerate 30 minutes. Roll pastry between sheets of plastic food wrap large enough to line a 23cm flan tin. Trim edges, prick well with a fork, bake in preheated CONVECTION oven 220°C for 15 minutes or until light golden brown, cool. Spread cold Orange Custard into flan, top with orange segments, brush with glaze. Refrigerate 1 hour before serving.

Orange Custard: Blend egg yolks, sugar and cornflour in a bowl with Grand Marnier and milk, cook on HIGH 4 minutes or until mixture boils and thickens, stirring once.

Beat soft cream cheese and orange rind in bowl until smooth, gradually beat in warm custard. (This can be done in an electric mixer or processor.) Place a piece of plastic food wrap over surface of custard, cool to room temperature.

Topping: Peel and segment oranges by cutting down between each segment next to membrane, over a bowl to catch juices. Drain segments on absorbent paper. Squeeze juice from remaining pulp into bowl. Add sugar and Grand Marnier to bowl, cook on HIGH 3 minutes or until mixture is thick and syrupy.

ALMOND APRICOT PEARS
2 firm pears, peeled, halved
2 tablespoons brandy
¼ cup water
2 tablespoons apricot jam
45g butter
¼ cup castor sugar
1 egg
1 cup (185g) ground almonds
2 sheets Ready Rolled Puff Pastry
1 egg, extra

Back: Walnut and Orange Cream Cheese Flan. Centre from left: Apple and Passionfruit Tart; Vanilla Passionfruit Slice. Front from left: Almond Apricot Pears; Wholemeal Carrot Flans.

Combine brandy, water and jam in bowl, cook on HIGH 1 minute, add cored pear halves, cook on HIGH 3 minutes or until just tender; baste once during cooking. Drain, reserve syrup, refrigerate pears until cold.

Cream butter, sugar and egg in small bowl of electric mixer; stir in almonds. Cut one sheet of pastry into 4 squares. Place each sheet between sheets of plastic food wrap, roll until larger and slightly thinner. Place a tablespoonful of almond mixture in centre of each pastry square, place a pear half, cut side up over centre, top with another tablespoonful of almond mixture. Spread with almond mixture evenly,

wrap pear in pastry, invert pears onto oven tray, mould pastry around shape of pear. From other sheet of pastry cut strips of pastry to represent "stems" of pears. Insert "stems" into ends of pears. Brush with beaten extra egg. Bake in pre-heated CONVECTION oven 220°C for 15 minutes or until light golden brown. Cook reserved syrup on HIGH 5 minutes or until slightly thick. Brush with syrup, sprinkle with almonds, serve with cream, icecream or custard.

Serves 4.

APPLE AND PASSIONFRUIT TART
125g butter
⅓ cup castor sugar
1 egg
1½ cups plain flour
½ cup self-raising flour
2 x 410g cans pie apple
½ cup lemon butter
2 passionfruit

Cream butter, sugar and egg on electric mixer until just combined. Stir in sifted flours, mix to a pliable dough. Cover, refrigerate 30 minutes. Roll three-quarters of the pastry large enough to line base and side of 20cm springform pan, to within 1cm from top of pan; trim neatly. Spread apples over base, top with combined lemon butter and passionfruit pulp. Roll scraps of remaining pastry into thin rectangular shape. Cut into strips, place over apples in lattice pattern, brush with a little milk. Bake in CONVECTION/MICROWAVE 180°C for 40 minutes. Stand 10 minutes before removing side of pan.

VANILLA PASSIONFRUIT SLICE
½ cup plain flour
½ cup custard powder
1 cup sugar
4½ cups milk
3 eggs
2 teaspoons vanilla
2 sheets Ready Rolled Puff Pastry
PASSIONFRUIT ICING
15g butter
1 tablespoon milk
2 passionfruit
1¾ cups icing sugar

Combine flour, custard powder and sugar in large bowl, gradually blend in milk, cook on HIGH 5 minutes or until mixture boils and thickens, stir twice during cooking. Stir in eggs and vanilla, cool, cover, refrigerate.
Place one sheet of pastry onto oven tray, bake in preheated CONVECTION oven 220°C for 12 minutes or until brown, turn onto wire rack to cool. Repeat with remaining pastry. Place one sheet of pastry, right side up, into 23cm square cake tin, lined with aluminium foil, trim if necessary. Spread with custard, top with remaining pastry, smooth side up. Spread with Passionfruit Icing, refrigerate several hours or overnight before cutting and serving.
Passionfruit Icing: Heat butter and milk in small bowl on HIGH 1 minute, stir in passionfruit pulp and sifted icing sugar, beat until smooth.

WHOLEMEAL CARROT FLANS
WHOLEMEAL PASTRY
½ cup wholemeal self-raising flour
½ cup white plain flour
90g butter
2 tablespoons brown sugar
1 egg yolk
1 tablespoon water, approximately
FILLING
⅓ cup pecan nuts
1½ cups grated carrot
1 tablespoon plain flour
¼ cup sultanas
2 tablespoons brown sugar
2 eggs
15g butter
3 tablespoons golden syrup

Wholemeal Pastry: Sift flours into basin, rub in butter, mix in sugar, add egg yolk and enough water to make a firm, pliable dough. Roll pastry out thinly, cut into 6 rounds large enough to line base and sides of 6 x 9cm flan tins. Pierce all over with fork, bake in preheated CONVECTION oven at 220°C, for 6 minutes, add Filling, decorate with reserved pecans, change setting to CONVECTION/MICROWAVE cook on 180°C, for 8 minutes, or until Filling has set.
Filling: Reserve 6 pecans for decorating flans, chop remaining nuts coarsely, mix with combined carrots, flour, sultanas, sugar, lightly beaten eggs, soft butter and golden syrup.

DESSERTS – HOT AND COLD

The desserts we've chosen for you range from the inexpensive family type to glamorous ones suitable for entertaining. We've made the most of using the microwave part of the oven, and then completed the main part of the cooking using the CONVECTION/MICROWAVE method. The rules are easy, cook as you would in a conventional oven, but reduce the cooking time. See the beginning of the Cakes section (page 95) for more details.

CARAMEL SELF-SAUCING PUDDING

1 cup brown sugar, lightly packed
2 teaspoons cornflour
1½ cups boiling water
30g butter
1 cup self-raising flour
½ cup castor sugar
¾ cup sultanas
½ cup milk
1 teaspoon vanilla

Blend brown sugar and cornflour with water and butter in dish (1 litre capacity). Cook on HIGH 3 minutes, stirring once during cooking. Sift flour and castor sugar into basin, stir in sultanas, milk and vanilla. Drop tablespoonfuls of mixture into hot caramel sauce in dish, bake in CONVECTION/MICROWAVE 180°C for 25 minutes, or until risen and golden brown. Serve warm with cream or ice cream.

Serves 4 to 6.

BLUEBERRY BUCKLE

A Canadian treat using blueberries,
(or any canned fruit of your choice).
It's like a self-saucing pudding.

60g butter
1 teaspoon grated lemon rind
½ cup sugar
1 egg
1 cup self-raising flour
⅓ cup milk
425g can blueberries
3 teaspoons cornflour
TOPPING
¼ cup ground almonds
¼ cup plain flour
¼ cup sugar
30g butter

Cream butter, lemon rind, sugar and egg until light and fluffy. Stir in sifted flour alternately with milk. Spread over base of 4 individual dishes (1-cup capacity). Drain blueberries, reserve syrup. Blend cornflour with reserved syrup, place in bowl, cook on HIGH 3 minutes. Stir in blueberries, spoon mixture into dishes, sprinkle with Topping, bake on CONVECTION/MICROWAVE 180°C for 15 minutes or until firm to touch. Serve warm with cream or ice cream.
Topping: Combine almonds, flour and sugar in bowl, rub in butter.
Serves 4.

ALMOND APPLE PUDDING

410g can pie apples
¼ teaspoon cinnamon
1 tablespoon castor sugar
125g butter
1 teaspoon grated lemon rind
½ cup brown sugar, firmly packed
2 eggs
1 cup self-raising flour
¼ cup ground almonds
2 tablespoons milk
1 tablespoon icing sugar
¼ teaspoon cinnamon, extra

Combine apples, cinnamon and castor sugar, spread into shallow dish (5-cup capacity). Cream butter, lemon rind and brown sugar in electric mixer, beat in eggs one at a time. Stir in sifted flour, almonds and milk. Spread over apples, cook on CONVECTION/MICROWAVE 180°C for 25 minutes, sprinkle with combined sifted icing sugar and extra cinnamon. Serve with whipped cream.
Serves 6.

LEFT:
Back from left: Blueberry Buckle;
Almond Apple Pudding. Front: Caramel
Self-Saucing Pudding.

ABOVE RIGHT:
Back: Chocolate Banana Souffle Pudding.
Front: Baked Carrot Pudding with Honey
Rum Sauce

BAKED CARROT PUDDING WITH HONEY RUM SAUCE

1 cup grated carrot
½ cup chopped dates
½ cup sultanas
½ cup currants
1 tablespoon chopped glace ginger
1 tablespoon mixed peel
125g butter
½ cup brown sugar, firmly packed
1 egg
1 cup self-raising wholemeal flour
½ teaspoon mixed spice
HONEY RUM SAUCE
1 cup brown sugar, lightly packed
¼ cup boiling water
½ cup honey
30g butter
1 teaspoon lemon juice
1 tablespoon rum

Combine carrot, dates, sultanas, currants, ginger and peel in a large bowl. Beat butter, sugar and egg until light and fluffy, stir into fruit mixture. Stir in sifted flour and spice. Spread into greased, base-lined loaf-shaped dish (base measures 10cm x 21cm) bake on CONVECTION/ MICROWAVE 180°C for 20 minutes or until firm to touch. Serve warm with Honey Rum Sauce.
Honey Rum Sauce: Combine sugar and water in bowl, stir until sugar is dissolved, add honey, butter and lemon juice, cook on HIGH 3 minutes, add rum.

CHOCOLATE BANANA SOUFFLE PUDDING

4 eggs, separated
¼ cup castor sugar
2 tablespoons plain flour
100g dark cooking chocolate, grated
2 ripe bananas, mashed
2 tablespoons rum

Combine egg yolks, sugar, flour, chocolate, bananas and rum in small bowl of electric mixer, beat 3 minutes or until mixture is smooth and changed in colour. Beat egg whites until soft peaks form, fold into chocolate mixture in two batches. Pour into 6 greased souffle dishes (1-cup capacity). Cook on CONVECTION/MICROWAVE 150°C for 10 minutes. Serve immediately, dusted with icing sugar and whipped cream if desired.
Serves 6.

CHOCOLATE ICECREAM CAKE

We used a special ring-shaped microwave proof pan for this recipe.

1 packet Chocolate Buttercake mix
⅓ cup water
1 litre carton vanilla icecream
100g packet Choc bits
½ cup Maple Flavored Syrup
1 tablespoon cream
¼ cup toasted flaked almonds (see note below)

Mix cake following directions on packet, then stir in water (this water is in addition to water specified in cake mix). Pour into greased and base-lined 20cm ring cake pan; cook on rack on CONVECTION/MICRO-WAVE 180°C for 20 minutes or until cake is firm and cooked through. Stand cake 5 minutes, turn onto wire rack to cool. Cut a quarter of the cake from the top, this forms a lid. Cut out centre of cake to within 1.5cm of side and base. This portion of cake is not needed for this recipe. Place cake on serving dish. Freeze cake 1 hour. Place icecream in bowl, cook on MEDIUM LOW 1 minute or until icecream is just beginning to soften, spread evenly into cake recess, place "lid" on top, freeze until solid, overnight if possible. Remove from freezer 30 minutes before serving. Place Choc bits and Maple Flavored Syrup in small bowl, cook on HIGH 1 minute, stir in cream, spoon over cake. Sprinkle with almonds.

Note: To toast flaked almonds, toast on oven tray in moderate oven 5 minutes; cool.

HAZELNUT AND CHOCOLATE TORTE

2 egg whites
½ cup castor sugar
125g roasted hazelnuts
2 tablespoons plain flour
CHOCOLATE CREAM
4 egg yolks
⅔ cup castor sugar
2 tablespoons cornflour
2 cups milk
100g dark cooking chocolate, chopped
2 teaspoons vanilla

Beat egg whites in small bowl of electric mixer until firm peaks form, gradually beat in sugar, beat until dissolved. Finely grind hazelnuts in processor or blender, combine with flour, fold gently into egg white mixture. Grease and flour 2 x 23cm bases of springform pans, spread mixture evenly over the two bases, smooth tops. Cook on two levels in pre-heated 180°C CONVECTION oven for 10 minutes, change position of cakes, cook further 10 minutes or until light golden brown and firm to touch. Cool 5 minutes, loosen gently from bases with knife, turn onto wire rack to cool.

STEP 1: Place a piece of plastic food wrap over one base of springform pan.

STEP 2: Place one layer of cake top side down over plastic. Pull edges of plastic wrap over cake.

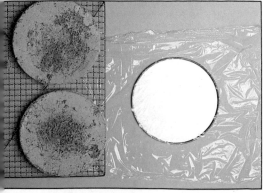

STRAWBERRY CREAM CHEESE FLAN

90g butter
185g packaged Nice biscuits, crushed
250g punnet strawberries, halved
2 passionfruit
2 tablespoons sugar
125g packet cream cheese
3 eggs
300 ml carton thickened cream
2 tablespoons lemon juice
¼ cup sugar, extra

Melt butter in bowl on HIGH 1 minute, stir in biscuit crumbs, press over base and side of deep 23cm flan tin. Combine strawberries with passionfruit and sugar, spread over base. Beat cream cheese in small bowl of electric mixer, add eggs, beat until smooth, beat in cream, lemon juice and extra sugar. Pour over strawberry mixture, bake on CONVECTION/MICROWAVE 180°C for 10 minutes or until set. When cold, decorate with extra whipped cream and strawberries if desired.

LEFT:
Left: Hazelnut and Chocolate Torte.
Right: Chocolate Icecream Cake

BELOW:
Strawberry Cream Cheese Flan

STEP 3: Place side of springform pan in place, secure with clip. Pull plastic wrap up and over side of tin, spread Chocolate Cream over cake, top with second layer of cake top side up. Refrigerate 1 hour, or until set. Release side of springform pan, invert cake onto serving plate, remove base and plastic wrap. Dust top with icing sugar and decorate as desired.

Chocolate Cream: Combine egg yolks, sugar and cornflour in bowl, gradually whisk in milk, cook on HIGH 6 minutes, or until sauce boils and thickens, stirring several times during cooking. Stir in chocolate and vanilla, beat until smooth, cover, refrigerate until cold.

APRICOT COCONUT PIE

125g butter
2 cups coconut
½ cup plain flour
¼ cup sugar
410g can pie apricots
¼ cup currants

Melt butter in bowl on HIGH 1 minute, stir in coconut, flour and sugar, press half the mixture into pie plate (base measures 18cm), top with combined apricots and currants. Sprinkle with remaining coconut mixture, cook on CONVECTION/ MICROWAVE 180°C for 30 minutes, or until browned. Stand 10 minutes, serve with cream.

COCONUT MERINGUE PIE

½ packet vanilla cake mix
2 cups milk
3 eggs, separated
⅔ cup castor sugar
2 teaspoons grated lemon rind
⅓ cup lemon juice
¾ cup coconut
½ cup castor sugar, extra

Prepare cake mix according to directions on packet (be sure to halve ingredients specified on packet). Pour into a greased pie plate (base measures 18cm), cook on HIGH 3 minutes, or until firm to touch, cool. When cold, crumble cake finely and combine with milk, egg yolks, sugar, lemon rind, lemon juice and coconut. Pour into greased, shallow 1.5 litre dish, cook on CONVECTION/MICROWAVE 180°C for 30 minutes or until set. Beat egg whites until soft peaks form, gradually beat in extra sugar, beat until dissolved. Spread over coconut mixture, cook on CONVEC-TION/MICROWAVE 180°C for 10 minutes or until lightly browned. Serve hot or cold with whipped cream.

From left: Apricot Coconut Pie; Coconut Meringue Pie

ROASTS

Meat roasted in a *CONVECTION/MICROWAVE oven looks the same as meat roasted in a conventional oven, the big advantage is the reduction in cooking time — about one third off the conventional method. Most CONVECTION/MICROWAVE ovens have a meat probe which gives accurate internal meat temperatures. Follow oven manufacturer's instructions for correct use.*

SWEET AND SOUR ROAST CHICKEN
Size 15 chicken
450g can pineapple pieces
3 green shallots, chopped
1 cup stale white breadcrumbs
1 tablespoon soy sauce
1 tablespoon vinegar
3 teaspoons cornflour
¼ cup water

Drain pineapple pieces, reserve syrup, combine pineapple, shallots and breadcrumbs, spoon into cavity of chicken. Secure openings of chicken with skewers, place breast side down on rack in baking dish. Brush with combined reserved pineapple syrup, soy sauce and vinegar. Cook on CONVECTION/MICROWAVE 180°C for 20 minutes, brushing occasionally with sauce. Turn chicken, cook further 40 minutes or until tender, brushing occasionally with sauce. Remove chicken from oven, wrap in aluminium foil, stand 10 minutes. Lift fat from pan juices, stir in blended cornflour and water. Cook on HIGH 3 minutes or until mixture boils and thickens, stirring once, serve over sliced chicken.
Serves 6.

COQ AU VIN IN A BAG
Size 15 chicken
⅓ cup plain flour
3 bacon rashers, chopped
2 onions, chopped
1 cup chicken stock
½ cup red wine
¼ cup brandy
2 tablespoons tomato paste
200g mushrooms, sliced

Place chicken into oven bag. Combine flour with bacon and onions in bowl, gradually blend in stock, red wine, brandy, tomato paste and mushrooms. Pour into bag with chicken, secure bag loosely with string or rubber band, place breast side down in dish. Cook on CONVECTION/MICROWAVE 180°C for 30 minutes, turn chicken over, cook further 30 minutes or until chicken is tender.
Serves 4.

Back: Sweet and Sour Roast Chicken.
Front: Coq au Vin in a Bag.

ROAST LEG OF PORK WITH SULTANA SAUCE

3kg leg of pork
salt
oil
SULTANA SAUCE
1 onion, grated
¾ cup dry apple cider
¼ cup dry white wine
1 cup beef stock
2 teaspoons french mustard
¼ cup red currant jelly
¾ cup sultanas
1 tablespoon cornflour
2 tablespoons port

Score rind of roast finely, rub with oil, then salt. Place roast on rack in baking dish, cook in preheated oven on CONVECTION 220°C for 20 minutes, change to CONVECTION/MICROWAVE 150°C, cook further 1½ hours or until tender, baste every 20 minutes. Stand 10 minutes before serving. It is easier to remove rind before slicing pork. Serve with Sultana Sauce.

Sultana Sauce: Combine onion, cider, wine, stock and mustard in a bowl. Cook on HIGH 10 minutes, stir in jelly, sultanas and blended cornflour and port. Cook on HIGH 5 minutes or until sauce boils and thickens.

Serves 8.

HONEY GLAZED TURKEY

Boil ½ cup pastina or risoni (rice-shaped pasta) in usual way for Seasoning.

3kg turkey
2 tablespoons honey
1 tablespoon soy sauce
1 tablespoon oil
SEASONING
15g butter
1 onion, chopped
1 clove garlic, crushed
2 teaspoons grated lemon rind
5 spinach leaves, finely shredded
1 cup cooked pastina or risoni
¾ cup stale breadcrumbs
2 tablespoons slivered almonds
2 bacon rashers, finely chopped

Wash turkey well, pat dry with absorbent paper. Spoon Seasoning into cavity of turkey, tuck wings under turkey, tie legs together with string. Place turkey in shallow dish, cook on CONVECTION/MICROWAVE 180°C for 45 minutes. Brush turkey with combined honey, soy sauce and oil, cook on CONVECTION/MICROWAVE 180°C a further hour, brushing frequently with honey mixture.

Seasoning: Combine butter, onion, garlic and lemon rind in bowl, cook on HIGH 2 minutes. Add spinach, cover, cook on HIGH 1 minute. Mix in pastina, breadcrumbs and almonds. Place bacon between sheets of absorbent paper, cook on HIGH 3 minutes, add to spinach mixture.

Serves 6.

116

HAM WITH APRICOT ORANGE GLAZE

905g can leg ham
whole cloves
½ cup apricot jam
1 tablespoon Grand Marnier
1 teaspoon french mustard
2 tablespoons orange juice

Place drained ham in baking dish, stud with cloves, brush with combined jam, Grand Marnier, mustard and orange juice. Cook on CONVECTION/MICROWAVE 150°C for 30 minutes, brush with glaze every 10 minutes. Decorate ham with strips of shallots, radish slices, red peppers and shredded orange rind.

Serves 4 to 6.

Back from left: Ham with Apricot Orange Glaze; Honey Glazed Turkey. Front from left: Roast Leg of Pork with Sultana Sauce; Duck Rolls with Orange Hazelnut Seasoning.

DUCK ROLLS WITH ORANGE HAZELNUT SEASONING

Size 18 duck
½ cup fresh orange juice
½ cup chicken stock
2 teaspoons cornflour
1 tablespoon Grand Marnier
ORANGE HAZELNUT SEASONING
30g butter
1 onion, finely chopped
2 cloves garlic, crushed
1 tablespoon Grand Marnier
¼ cup finely chopped roasted hazelnuts
2 teaspoons grated orange rind
1½ cups stale wholemeal breadcrumbs
1 egg

STEP 1: Cut duck down backbone, cut meat away from rib cage, remove, leave wings and legs intact.

STEP 2: Remove first two joints from wings. Cut meat away from remaining wing bones, remove bones.

STEP 3: Cut off ends of drumsticks (a cleaver will do this easily). Cut meat away from thigh and drumstick bones, remove bones. Trim excess fat.

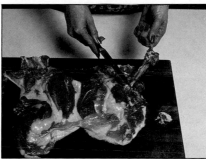

STEP 4: Cut boned duck in half between the breast fillets. Trim all fat from duck, trim skin around edges. Divide Orange Hazelnut Seasoning between each half. Roll up, starting at breast fillet end, so it is protected in the middle during cooking.

STEP 5: Tie rolls with string in several places, place on rack over shallow baking dish. Cook on CONVECTION/MICROWAVE 180°C for 40 minutes. Drain all but 1 tablespoon of fat from dish, add orange juice, blended stock and cornflour and Grand Marnier, cook on HIGH 5 minutes, stir once during cooking; strain. Remove string from rolls, serve sliced with sauce.

Orange Hazelnut Seasoning: Combine butter, onion and garlic in bowl, cook on HIGH 3 minutes, stir in Grand Marnier, hazelnuts, orange rind, breadcrumbs and lightly beaten egg.
Serves 4 to 6.

CRUSTY LEG OF LAMB WITH TOMATO SAUCE

1.75 kg leg of lamb
CRUST
3 cups stale breadcrumbs
2 tablespoons chopped basil (or 1 teaspoon dried basil leaves)
2 cloves garlic, crushed
125g butter, softened
TOMATO SAUCE
1 onion, chopped
2 cloves garlic, crushed
400g can tomatoes
1 teaspoon sugar
1 tablespoon chopped parsley
1 teaspoon worcestershire sauce
⅓ cup dry white wine
3 teaspoons cornflour

Place lamb in shallow dish, fat side up, cook on CONVECTION/MICROWAVE 150°C for 45 minutes, drain, reserve 1 tablespoon fat from dish. Remove surface fat from lamb, pat Crust on firmly, cook further 15 minutes in CONVECTION oven 220°C for 15 minutes or until Crust has browned. Remove from oven, stand 15 minutes before slicing and serving with Tomato Sauce.

Crust: Combine all ingredients.

Tomato Sauce: Cook onion and garlic in bowl with reserved fat on HIGH 4 minutes. Add undrained crushed tomatoes, sugar, parsley, worcestershire sauce and blended wine and cornflour, cook further 5 minutes on HIGH or until Sauce boils and thickens slightly.

Serves 6.

Back: Crusty Leg of Lamb with Tomato Sauce. Front from left: Racks of Lamb Wellington Style; Loin of Lamb with Feta Cheese and Spinach Seasoning.

RACKS OF LAMB WELLINGTON STYLE

2 racks of lamb (8 cutlets in each)
4 cloves garlic, peeled
2 teaspoons dried rosemary leaves
1 tablespoon mint jelly
3 sheets Ready Rolled Puff Pastry
1 egg
SAUCE
15g butter
1 tablespoon plain flour
1 teaspoon french mustard
1 tablespoon brandy
1 cup beef stock

Trim fat from lamb. Cut garlic into quarters lengthways; insert slivers between cutlets on racks. Place mint jelly in small dish, cook on HIGH 30 seconds or until melted, brush over lamb; sprinkle with rosemary. Place lamb into flat dish, cook on CONVECTION/MICROWAVE 180°C for 20 minutes, baste during cooking. Reserve pan juices; refrigerate lamb until cold. Wrap both cold lamb racks separately in a sheet of puff pastry. Cut remaining pastry into thin strips, twist strips around bones. Brush pastry with beaten egg, place onto round oven tray, place on rack in oven, cook on CONVECTION 230°C for 20 minutes or until pastry is golden brown and cooked. Place reserved pan juices in bowl with butter, cook on HIGH 30 seconds or until butter is melted, stir in flour, mustard, brandy and stock, beat well, cook on HIGH 3 minutes or until sauce boils and thickens; strain and serve with sliced racks of lamb.

Serves 6.

LOIN OF LAMB WITH FETA CHEESE AND SPINACH SEASONING

2 x 750g loins of lamb, boned
SEASONING
250g packet frozen spinach, thawed
125g mushrooms, sliced
4 green shallots, chopped
2 cloves garlic, crushed
15g butter
1 cup stale breadcrumbs
1 tablespoon chopped fresh dill (or ½ teaspoon dried dill leaves)
1 tablespoon chopped parsley
60g feta cheese
SAUCE
¼ cup dry white wine
2 teaspoons cornflour
1 tablespoon sugar
3 green shallots, chopped
¼ cup chopped parsley
½ cup chopped mint
1 cup chicken stock
1 tablespoon finely chopped mint, extra

Trim fat from lamb, lay out flat, spread on Seasoning, roll up, tie securely, place on rack in baking dish, fat side up, cook on CONVECTION/MICROWAVE 150°C for 30 minutes or until lamb is tender. Remove lamb from pan, stand 10 minutes before slicing and serving with Sauce.

Seasoning: Press as much liquid as possible from spinach. Combine mushrooms, shallots, garlic and butter in bowl, cook on HIGH 3 minutes, stir in breadcrumbs, dill, parsley, crumbled cheese and spinach.

Sauce: Combine blended wine and cornflour, sugar, shallots, parsley, mint and stock, add to baking dish (if microwave proof). Cook on HIGH 5 minutes or until Sauce boils and thickens. Stir in extra mint.

Serves 6 to 8.

LOIN OF VEAL WITH ANCHOVY SEASONING

You might have to order a loin of veal from the butcher. Ask him to bone it out for you and to leave as much flap as possible.

1kg boned loin of veal
30g butter
½ cup red wine
1 cup beef stock
1 tablespoon chopped parsley
1 clove garlic, crushed
2 teaspoons grated lemon rind
2 teaspoons cornflour
2 tablespoons water
ANCHOVY SEASONING
45g can anchovies, drained
100g prosciutto, chopped
1 tablespoon capers, chopped
1 clove garlic, crushed
1 tablespoon chopped parsley
2 tablespoons tomato paste
15g butter
1 cup stale wholemeal breadcrumbs

Open loin of veal out flat, place Seasoning along thickest part of meat, roll up, tie with string in several places; place on rack over large dish, dot with butter. Combine wine and stock, pour over veal. Cook on CONVECTION/MICROWAVE 180°C for 1 hour. Combine garlic, parsley and lemon rind, sprinkle over veal, cook on CONVECTION/MICROWAVE 180°C for 15 minutes. Blend cornflour and water, stir into pan juices, cook on HIGH 3 minutes or until sauce boils and thickens, serve over sliced meat.

Anchovy Seasoning: Soak anchovies in water 10 minutes, drain, chop finely. Combine anchovies in bowl with prosciutto, capers, garlic, parsley, tomato paste and soft butter, mix well, add breadcrumbs, mix well.

Serves 6 to 8.

LOIN OF PORK WITH LEEK AND APRICOT SEASONING

Ask butcher to bone out loin of pork for you and to leave a flap.

2kg loin of pork, boned
30g butter
2 leeks, sliced
1 clove garlic, crushed
1 cup (125g) dried apricots
2 teaspoons curry powder
1 teaspoon salt

Remove rind and all fat from pork, spread pork out flat. Combine butter, leeks and garlic in bowl, cook on HIGH 5 minutes; drain well. Place apricots in bowl, cover with hot water, cook on HIGH 3 minutes; drain well. Spread leek mixture over inside of pork, place apricots down centre, fold pork over, tie with string at 2.5cm intervals. Rub skin with combined curry powder and salt. Place pork in baking dish, cook on CONVECTION/MICROWAVE 180°C for 1 hour or until tender.

Serves 6.

BEEF WITH HAM AND MANGO CHUTNEY SEASONING

1kg beef eye-fillet, in one piece
15g butter
1 small onion, chopped
1 clove garlic, crushed
250g ham, finely minced
1 cup stale white breadcrumbs
1 tablespoon mango chutney
2 tablespoons chopped parsley
1 tablespoon oil

Insert a sharp knife lengthwise through centre of beef. Combine butter, onion and garlic in bowl, cook on HIGH 3 minutes. Mix in ham, breadcrumbs, chutney and parsley. Spoon seasoning into beef, using handle of wooden spoon to push seasoning into centre of beef. Tie beef at 2.5cm intervals with string, rub beef with oil. Place beef in dish, cook on CONVECTION/MICROWAVE 180°C for 40 minutes for medium rare, or about 5 minutes longer for well done steak.

Serves 4 to 6.

SEASONED TOPSIDE ROLL WITH SOUR CREAM SAUCE

8cm thick slice topside steak (about 1.25kg)
100g ham, thinly sliced
100g salami, thinly sliced
1½ cups stale breadcrumbs
¼ cup grated parmesan cheese
2 green shallots, chopped
1 egg
SOUR CREAM SAUCE
300g carton sour cream
2 teaspoons grainy mustard

Use sharp knife to cut meat almost through horizontally or ask butcher to "butterfly" meat for you. Open meat out flat, pound slightly with mallet, top evenly with ham and salami slices. Combine breadcrumbs with cheese, shallots and egg, press on top of sliced meat. Roll up tightly like a swiss roll, tie at 2.5cm intervals with string. Place in baking dish, cook on CONVECTION/MICROWAVE 180°C for 40 minutes or until meat is tender. Meat will remain pink inside due to color of ham and salami. Serve sliced, hot or cold with Sour Cream Sauce.

Sour Cream Sauce: Mix ingredients together thoroughly.

Serves 6 to 8.

Back from left: Loin of Veal with Anchovy Seasoning; Loin of Pork with Leek and Apricot Seasoning. Front from left: Beef with Ham and Mango Chutney Seasoning; Seasoned Topside Roll with Sour Cream Sauce.

DINNER PARTY FOR TWO

Quail is deliciously tender and easy to eat when the rib-cage has been removed. It is simple to do, and well worth the little extra effort to impress that special person. Follow our steps and guide to make the dinner party flow along without a hitch.

- *Make Tomato Sauce for quail the day before party, cover, refrigerate.*
- *Bone and stuff quail the morning of the party.*
- *Make sauce for oysters in the afternoon. Pour sauce over oysters when ready to serve.*
- *Complete Tartlets up to 4 hours before serving.*
- *Top and tail 60g snow peas, place in shallow dish.*
- *First cook potatoes for 20 minutes on high rack, then add quail to low rack, continue cooking quail and potatoes for remaining specified cooking time.*
- *Reheat Tomato Sauce in shallow dish on HIGH 3 minutes. Serve with snow peas.*
- *Cook snow peas last. Add 1 tablespoon water to snow peas, cover, cook on HIGH 3 minutes.*

MENU

Hot Creamy Oysters

Seasoned Quail with Tomato Sauce

Baby Parmesan Potatoes

Strawberry Grand Marnier Tartlets

HOT CREAMY OYSTERS
12 oysters on the shell
1 clove garlic, crushed
1 green shallot, chopped
15g butter
2 teaspoons cornflour
2 tablespoons dry white wine
½ cup cream
1 egg yolk
⅓ cup grated tasty cheese
TOPPING
1 slice wholemeal bread, toasted
2 teaspoons chopped parsley
1 tablespoon grated parmesan cheese
2 teaspoons soft butter
1 teaspoon lemon juice

Combine garlic, shallot and butter in bowl, cook on HIGH 2 minutes, stir in blended cornflour and wine, then cream, cook on HIGH 3 minutes or until mixture boils and thickens. Stir once during cooking. Stir in egg yolk and cheese, stir until cheese is melted. Pour sauce over oysters in the shell. Sprinkle with Topping, cook on CONVECTION/MICROWAVE 180° for 10 minutes or until sauce is bubbly. Serve immediately.

Topping: Crumble toast finely, combine with parsley and cheese in bowl, mix in butter and lemon juice.

BABY PARMESAN POTATOES
6 baby potatoes
½ cup oil
2 tablespoons grated parmesan cheese

Peel potatoes, trim to a smooth round shape. Cut a slice from base of potatoes, so potatoes sit flat. Make cuts 2mm apart through to base (do not cut all the way through). Place into dish with ¼ cup of the oil, cook on high rack on CONVECTION/MICROWAVE 180°C for 30 minutes. Brush with remaining oil during cooking. Sprinkle with cheese, cook further 10 minutes or until potatoes are tender.

STEP 1: Run knife down both sides of rib-cage of each quail.

STEP 2: Carefully cut away rib-cage from flesh; leave wings and legs intact.

STRAWBERRY GRAND MARNIER TARTLETS

PASTRY
½ cup plain flour
1 tablespoon icing sugar
1 egg yolk
30g soft butter
FILLING
2 tablespoons custard powder
½ cup sugar
¾ cup milk
1 egg
1 tablespoon Grand Marnier
30g butter
TOPPING
250g punnet strawberries, halved
1 teaspoon gelatine
3 teaspoons water
1 tablespoon red currant jelly
2 teaspoons Grand Marnier

Pastry: Sift flour and icing sugar into bowl, quickly mix in egg yolk and butter with fingertips. Press evenly over base and sides of 2 individual flan dishes (base measures 11cm), pierce well with fork. Bake in preheated oven CONVECTION 200°C for 10 minutes or until golden; cool.

Filling: Combine custard powder and sugar in bowl, stir in combined milk and beaten egg. Cook on HIGH 3 minutes or until mixture boils and thickens, stirring occasionally; add Grand Marnier, refrigerate covered. Cream butter in small bowl of electric mixer until light and fluffy, gradually beat in cold custard, beating well after each addition.

Topping: Sprinkle gelatine over water in cup, stir, cook on HIGH 30 seconds or until gelatine is dissolved. Stir in red currant jelly and Grand Marnier, cool, do not allow to set. Divide Filling between pastry cases, top with strawberries, brush with glaze, refrigerate 30 minutes before serving.

SEASONED QUAIL WITH TOMATO SAUCE

You will need to boil ⅓ cup brown rice in conventional way for Seasoning.

4 large quail
1 tablespoon oil
SEASONING
1 bacon rasher, chopped
1 cup cooked brown rice
2 tablespoons chopped parsley
3 green shallots, chopped
2 tablespoons parmesan cheese
TOMATO SAUCE
15g butter
1 onion, chopped
1 carrot, chopped
1 clove garlic, crushed
1 bacon rasher, chopped
2 tomatoes, chopped
2 teaspoons tomato paste
½ cup chicken stock
1 tablespoon dry sherry
2 teaspoons cornflour

Remove rib-cages from quail, as shown. Spoon seasoning down centre of each quail, fold one side over and then the other. Sew flesh together using needle and dark thread. Tie quail with string. Place quail in shallow dish, brush with oil, cook on CONVECTION/MICROWAVE 180°C for 20 minutes. Serve with Tomato Sauce.

Seasoning: Place bacon between sheets of absorbent paper, cook on HIGH 2 minutes. Combine bacon, rice, parsley, shallots and cheese.

Tomato Sauce: Combine butter, onion, carrot, garlic and bacon in bowl, cover, cook on HIGH 3 minutes. Add tomatoes, tomato paste and stock, cover, cook on HIGH 12 minutes; strain. Stir in blended sherry and cornflour, cook on HIGH 2 minutes or until Sauce boils and thickens. Stir once during cooking.

DINNER PARTY FOR SIX

Prepare the dessert and entree the morning of the dinner party, the final assembly of the entree must be left until about an hour before the guests arrive.

- Marinate veal overnight.
- Coffee Walnut Sponge Torte can be made and assembled the morning of the party.
- The 3 vegetables for the Terrine can be prepared the morning of the party and assembled an hour before guests arrive.
- Cook veal for 30 minutes, remove from oven while cooking Terrine. Continue to cook veal (with marinade) while Terrine is standing.
- Boil tagliatelle in conventional way.
- Boil or steam broccoli in conventional way.

MENU

Rainbow Vegetable Terrine

Green Peppercorn Nut of Veal with Tomato Sauce

Tagliatelle

Broccoli

Coffee Walnut Sponge Torte

GREEN PEPPERCORN NUT OF VEAL WITH TOMATO SAUCE

1kg nut of veal
1 tablespoon french mustard
55g can green peppercorns, drained
2 cloves garlic, crushed
1 cup dry white wine
2 bacon rashers
3 tomatoes, peeled, chopped
2 teaspoons cornflour
1 tablespoon water
2 tablespoons chopped parsley

Combine mustard, crushed peppercorns, garlic and wine in shallow dish, add veal, coat well, cover, marinate overnight in refrigerator. Place veal onto roasting rack, cover with bacon. Stand rack over dish of marinade on turntable. Cook on CONVECTION/MICROWAVE 180°C for 30 minutes, mix tomatoes into marinade, return marinade to oven (underneath meat), cook 30 minutes on CONVECTION/MICROWAVE 180°C or until veal is tender. Remove meat from oven, cover, stand while finishing sauce. Stir blended cornflour and water into tomato mixture, cook on HIGH 5 minutes or until sauce boils and thickens, stir in parsley. Serve veal thinly sliced with tomato sauce.

RAINBOW VEGETABLE TERRINE

Use old style pumpkin for this recipe, not the softer butternut or golden nugget variety.

400g pumpkin, peeled
¾ cup thickened cream
3 cloves garlic
500g mushrooms, chopped
8 spinach leaves
pinch nutmeg
1½ cups (185g) grated tasty cheese
6 eggs

Chop pumpkin roughly, then chop finely in processor, place in bowl with ¼ cup of the cream and 1 clove of the crushed garlic, cook on HIGH 10 minutes; cool.

Chop mushrooms finely in processor, place in bowl with another ¼ cup of the cream and another clove of the crushed garlic, cook on HIGH 8 minutes, drain, press out as much liquid as possible; cool.

Chop spinach finely in processor, place in bowl with nutmeg, remaining ¼ cup cream and remaining crushed clove of garlic, cook on HIGH 5 minutes, drain, press out as much liquid as possible; cool.

Beat 2 eggs and ⅓ of the cheese in 3 separate bowls; add pumpkin to one, mushrooms to another and spinach to another, mix well. Spread spinach evenly into greased loaf tin (base measures 10cm x 22cm), top evenly with pumpkin layer, then with mushroom layer, cook on low rack on CONVECTION/MICROWAVE 150°C for 30 minutes. Place strips of aluminium foil around top edge where already cooked, cook further 10 minutes or until centre is firm and set. Stand 10 minutes. Loosen edges with a knife, turn onto serving plate, serve warm in slices.

COFFEE WALNUT SPONGE TORTE
SPONGE
3 eggs
½ cup castor sugar
¾ cup self-raising flour
2 tablespoons cornflour
½ cup finely chopped walnuts
1 teaspoon butter
3 tablespoons hot water
1 tablespoon Tia Maria
1 teaspoon instant coffee powder
1 tablespoon hot water, extra
COFFEE CREAM
2 x 300ml cartons thickened cream
2 teaspoons instant coffee powder
2 tablespoons Tia Maria

Sponge: Beat eggs in small bowl of electric mixer until thick and creamy, gradually beat in sugar, beat until dissolved. Sift flour and cornflour together several times. Melt butter in hot water. Transfer egg mixture to a large bowl, sift flours over egg mixture, fold in lightly with walnuts, then fold in butter and water. Spread into greased base-lined deep 20cm cake tin, cook on CONVECTION/ MICROWAVE 150°C for 15 minutes or until cake feels firm to touch. Turn onto wire rack to cool.

Split cold cake into two layers, brush layers with combined Tia Maria, coffee powder and extra hot water. Place one layer of cake onto serving plate, spread with ⅓ of the Coffee Cream, top with remaining layer of cake. Spread top and sides of cake with remaining Coffee Cream. If desired, decorate with strawberries, kiwi fruit and walnuts.

Coffee Cream: Dissolve coffee in Tia Maria, fold into whipped cream.

INDEX

127

CONVECTION

CREDITS

Austfloyd Pty Ltd — Fitz & Floyd China
Casa Shopping
Crown Corning Ltd.
Elof Hansson (Aust.) Pty. Ltd. — Cutlery
Ferguson's Garden Centres
Fred Pazotti Pty. Ltd. — Tiles
Gelosa Kitchens — Cover Kitchen
Gibbs Bright & Co. Pty. Ltd. — Wilsonart
H.A.G. Import Corpn. (Australia) Pty. Ltd. —
    Glassware
Josiah Wedgwood & Sons (Aust.) Pty. Ltd.
Kosta-Boda Aust. Pty. Ltd.
Laminex Industries
Mikasa Tableware (N.S.W.) Pty. Ltd.
National Panasonic (Aust.) Pty. Ltd.
Noritake (Aust.) Pty. Ltd.
Orrefors Australia Pty. Ltd.
Phillip Lazarus Pty. Ltd. — China
Shea & Associates — Holmegaard Glassware
Shorters — Tableware
Swift Consumer Products — Thomas China
Swiss-Anglo — Spode China
Vasa Agencies (Aust.) Pty. Ltd. — Bodum
    Glassware
Villeroy & Boch (Aust.) Pty. Ltd.